Prologue

It's so cold in here. The chill seems to seep into my bones, making me shiver despite the sweat that clings to my skin. The sterile smell of disinfectant hangs in the air, sharp and uninviting, mixing with the faint clinical scent of antiseptic that seems to permeate everything. It's the kind of smell that settles deep in your memory, forever associated with fear and uncertainty. The continuous beeping of the machines is starting to sound like the soundtrack from a horror film. Each beep a sharp, jarring reminder of the fragility of life—of her life.

The rhythmic sound, meant to monitor her well-being, now feels like a ticking clock, counting down to something I can't control. I'm sweating, but not from heat. Each breath I take is getting harder and harder, as if an invisible weight is pressing on my chest, making it impossible to breathe deeply, to think clearly. I try to focus on the steady rise and fall of her chest, but even that small task feels tedious.

When I look at her, lying there so still, a rush of emotions crashes over me like a tidal wave: sadness, hurt, anxiety, and frustration, all tangled together in a knot that I can't seem to untie. The sight of her like this, so vulnerable, breaks something inside me.And still, there's this flicker of frustration, a tiny flame that I try desperately to snuff out.

How can I be frustrated with her during a time like this? What kind of person does that make me?

The thought lodges itself in my mind, no matter how hard I try to push it away. It lingers, nibbling at the edges of my conscience, making me question everything—my feelings, my reactions, my own humanity. As I sit here, fighting to hold it all together, I can't help but feel like I'm coming apart at the seams.

I have to use the bathroom so badly, but I finally got her to calm down and rest. My mother's breathing has steadied, and the tension in her face has eased just a bit. Her honey-brown skin, usually so warm and vibrant, looked pale under the fluorescent light. The years had left their mark on her delicate features; her sad, almond-shaped eyes, framed by thin lashes, seemed to carry the weight of every struggle she had endured.

Her long, thin hair, once a source of pride, now lay limp against the pillow, a few stray strands sticking to her damp forehead. The big nose that had always defined her face now looks softer somehow. Her thin lips, often pressed into a tight line of worry, now parted slightly as she rested.

I really don't want to move my hand from under her arm and wake her. The warmth of her skin against mine is the only thing keeping me grounded, like an anchor tethering me to this moment, and her. I feel the rhythmic rise and fall of her chest, a quiet reassurance that she's still here with me. The soft hum of the machines in the background is a stark contrast to the chaos that brews inside me, but as long as she's at peace, I can keep it together.

I glance at the clock on the wall, the dim light casting shadows that stretch and warp with each passing minute. The minutes crawl by, each second marked by the relentless ticking that echoes through the silence of the room. It's strange how time seems to distort in moments like this, where everything else fades away. It's just her and I, suspended in this bubble of time, amidst the cold and the beeping and the unspoken fears that linger in the air like a heavy fog. I can't help but think back to all the times we've been here before, and all the battles we've fought. As I sit here, holding onto her, memories from the past begin to surface, pulling me back into the whirlwind of everything that led us to this moment.

Let me take you back to the beginning and give you some back story.

Chapter One: Strangers Under One Roof

Growing up as the second to last of seven children in a family where closeness was a luxury we didn't have, I often found myself caught in the gap between generations. My older sisters, already adults by the time I was forming my earliest memories, had moved out, leaving behind echoes of their presence but little else. In our large family, you'd think the house would be filled with noise, laughter, and shared experiences, but instead, it was more like a collection of individuals living separate lives under one roof. We were a typical African American family in the mid 80's, growing up in the "hood" with limited resources.

We were strangers to both sides of our extended family. To this day, I still don't know why we never went to family reunions or met anyone from my mother's side. It was a mystery I never had the chance to solve. Occasionally, we spent time with my father's side of the family, but even those visits were rare. I never met my dad, but the time spent with my paternal grandmother and other relatives offered brief glimpses into what could have been a different life—a life with family ties that extended beyond the walls of our home. These moments, however fleeting, were like fragments of another reality, a life I could observe but never fully be a part of.

My mother gave birth to me when she was 36 years old, already seasoned in the trials of life and motherhood. By then, she had been married to my father, but they separated shortly after I was born. My three brothers—Larry, Lamar, and Lionel— and I had the same father, while my sisters, Patricia and Diane, had another dad. Our youngest sibling, Toshianna, had her own father too. It was a patchwork family, with each of us connected by blood but divided by different histories and the men who had come and gone.

My mother wasn't the affectionate type. In our house, love was something you had to assume, not something that was spoken aloud or demonstrated through hugs and words. She was more of a "you should know I love you" type, believing that her intentions and actions were enough to convey what she couldn't say. But as a child, that unspoken love often felt like an absence, a void where comfort and security should have been.

She had a way of making decisions that seemed irrational to everyone but her. One of her favorite sayings was, "God will take care of us," a mantra she repeated with unwavering conviction. To an outsider, it might have sounded like she had unshakable faith, but for us, it was the prelude to yet another struggle. She would refuse to pay the rent, giving all her money to the church instead, confident that divine intervention would keep us safe and secure.

But faith alone couldn't prevent the inevitable. God took care of us, she'd say, as we packed up our belongings—whatever we could fit into our backpacks—and caught the city bus to the nearest homeless shelter. I felt like it was her way of showing us that faith could carry us through anything, even if it meant living on the edge of survival.

I later discovered that my mother hadn't been entirely truthful about always giving her money to the church. While she did pay her tithes most of the time, a significant portion of her money went to her drug-addicted boyfriend. Maybe she thought blaming the church was an easier story to tell, something less shameful than admitting she was supporting his addiction. But that lie planted a deep seed of mistrust in me.

I couldn't understand why she would sacrifice so much for someone who gave nothing in return. Worse, I couldn't fathom how she could claim it was all in service to God when we were struggling so badly. We went without basic necessities while she claimed she was "giving to the Lord." In my young mind, the church was the place that took what little we had and left us with nothing.

It wasn't long before I began to resent anything related to religion. To me, churches weren't houses of faith; they were businesses exploiting people like my mother. Preachers became symbols of greed, collecting offerings while their congregations went hungry. I hated the idea of tithes and offerings, seeing them as nothing more than manipulative schemes.

When I was about five or six, I remembered my uncle coming to Minnesota to pick up my brothers for the summer. They were going to spend the break in Illinois with our grandma, and I wasn't part of the plans. But my mom begged him to take me along. It was a last-minute decision—so last-minute that she didn't even pack any clothes for me. I spent that summer wearing my brothers' clothes, including a pair of penny loafers that were too big and not meant for a little girl. We still laugh about those shoes, but the truth is, it wasn't funny back then.

That summer trip turned into a couple of years. My mom never came back to get us. I remember calling her, begging her to pick us up. She would always say she'd be there the next weekend, and I would wait. I'd stare out the window every ten minutes, my heart racing at every car that passed by, hoping it was her. I was too afraid to leave the house, scared I'd miss her if I wasn't there when she arrived. But she never came. She was always somewhere else, and we were always waiting.

When she finally came to get us, two years later, I could barely contain my excitement. The moment I saw her car pull up, I bolted toward it, my heart racing with happiness. I flung open the door, ready to throw my arms around her, but then I froze. There, sitting in the backseat, was a little girl. She had chubby cheeks, big brown eyes, and a curious expression.

"Who's that?" I asked, glancing from her to my mother, confused.

My mom turned around, her voice casual, like this was the most normal thing in the world. "That's your sister, Toshianna."

I blinked, staring at the child. "My sister?"

"Yeah," my mom said. "She's three. You remember her, don't you?"

But I didn't. I didn't remember her at all. It felt like I was meeting her for the first time, even though she must have been born before I left.

How could I not remember my own sister?

She was different. She talked funny, made strange hand movements in front of her face, and smiled a lot. I didn't understand it then, but I would later learn that she was developmentally delayed.

The unsteady beeping of the heart monitor pulls me back into the sterile hospital room. I lean over, glancing at my mother. She lays still, her chest rising and falling in soft, rhythmic breaths, her lips part ever so slightly as she sleeps. Her face looks peaceful, so at odds with the noise of the heart monitor that seems to scream otherwise.

Congestive heart failure is just one of the many things that weighs on her body, yet somehow, despite the constant threat of her heart giving out, she manages to rest. The monitor lets out another sharp beep—louder this time, longer—but like before, the numbers stabilize, the sounds fade, and calm returns. I know by now not to panic every time it happens, but my heart still skips a beat with every alarm. The sharpness of that sound has a way of twisting my insides, reminding me how delicate everything is.

She stirs slightly, letting out a soft snore that reassures me. Her body, frail as it is, still finds rest. That sound, the tiny rumble of a light snore, is oddly comforting. I sigh, adjusting myself in the stiff hospital chair next to her bed, the vinyl squeaking beneath me.

I think about how often we have found ourselves here, in these cold rooms with their unyielding fluorescent lights, the soft hum of machines tracking her every breath, every heartbeat. This isn't new. Yet somehow, every visit feels like a fragile balance between hope and fear—hope that she might recover, fear that she might not.

As I settle deeper into my chair, my body relaxes, and my thoughts wander. The periodic beeping fades into the background like a clock, and I drift, not into sleep, but into memories. Memories of her as she was before the sickness, memories of a time when it was her that was supposed to be watching over me, not the other way around.

***

We spent most of our elementary school years caught in a cycle of instability, moving in and out of shelters and staying with friends of my mother. Our life was a series of temporary fixes, each one promising some semblance of stability but always ending in another move, another goodbye. When we did have our own place, it never lasted long. One irrational decision after another kept us uprooted, living out of bags and boxes, never quite settling in.

Despite the chaos, my mother worked hard. She was a daycare teacher, and I watched her get up and go to work every day, no matter what was happening at home. It's part of the reason I could never understand why we moved around so much.

If she was so dedicated to her job, why couldn't we stay in one place? Why did we have to live like this?

We lived in Minnesota; my mom had moved all of us there when I was just a baby. My older sister Trish didn't come with us—she was about 14 and pregnant with my niece, so she stayed behind in Illinois. Diane moved to Las Vegas with my dad when he left my mom. So, it was just my mom, my three brothers, and me.

By the time I entered middle school, the idea of things finally turning around seemed within reach. My mom had secured housing assistance, and we moved into a big four-bedroom house in North Minneapolis. The space felt like a luxury we hadn't known before, and for a fleeting moment, I allowed myself to believe that this could be the start of something better, something more stable. We had a house, a place we could call our own. It felt like it could be permanent, like maybe, just maybe, we could finally become a "normal" family.

But normalcy, like stability, remained an illusion.

Despite the new house, the security it should have brought never materialized. My mom, while present enough to make sure we were ready for church on Sundays, was conspicuously absent the rest of the week. It was as if the house existed in two parallel realities—one where the façade of normalcy was upheld for a few hours in church on Sunday mornings, and another where my brothers and I were left to fend for ourselves.

Church wasn't just a routine; it was my mother's lifeline. She believed deeply that as long as she appeared devout, as long as she showed up every Sunday dressed in her finest, God would somehow provide or forgive the instability at home. In her mind, church attendance was a shield—a way to ward off the judgment of the outside world and a way to show that despite everything, she was trying. The appearance of being a good Christian was crucial to her, even if the rest of our lives were crumbling behind closed doors.

For my mother, faith was intertwined with survival. I think she needed to believe that her devotion would bring some sense of order to the chaos we lived in.

We would go days without seeing her.

What was she doing? Where was she?

No one seemed to know, or maybe no one dared to ask. In her absence, my brothers—left without guidance or structure—found trouble easily. The lure of the streets, the temptation to fall into bad crowds, was too strong when no one was there to rein them in.

I remember clearly a time when Lionel and I had to strategize how we could intercept our mom before she started spending, crouched in the hallway, whispering like we were planning some kind of secret operation.

"Okay, look," Lionel said, glancing at the clock. "She gets off at 5:30pm. If we dip now, we can catch the bus before she does and meet her at the stop."

"But what if she…

He quickly cut me off, "Just come on man," he said, determined. "If we don't get down there, we gon' be burnt up."

I nodded, thinking of the empty fridge and the nearly finished bar of soap in the bathroom.

"Aight, cool let's go." I said, grabbing my backpack.

As we raced out the door, my heart pounded, knowing that this might be our only chance to catch her. We were on a mission, hoping to intercept her paycheck before it disappeared, leaving us scrambling for the basics all over again.

These were battles we fought weekly. School clothes were something we got at the start of the year, and if we grew out of them, too bad. We had to make them last, patching up the holes and squeezing into shoes that were too small. If they didn't fit, we just had to deal with it. The next school year was the only hope for replacements.

As soon as my oldest brother Larry was old enough, he couldn't wait to escape. The whirlwind of chaos that defined our lives was too much, and he saw his chance for something different—a life that wasn't tied to the dysfunction we had come to accept. He took off to Las Vegas, to live with our dad, lured by the promise of a fresh start and stability. It was hard to blame him. The pull to find a way out was strong, and he wasn't the only one who felt it. When Lamar turned 18, he followed a similar path, enlisting in the military to escape. For him, the uniform, the discipline, and the structure of the military must have felt like the complete opposite of the life we knew. It became order where there had only been chaos.

As each of them left, it felt like our family was slowly unraveling, one sibling at a time. We were each looking for our own escape from the disarray that had become our lives. While they were able to leave, I was left behind, caught in the madness that seemed impossible to escape from. My mom would never allow me to go be with my dad. I was sad, but going to Las Vegas with my dad wasn't an option for me. As a child, I didn't understand why. I'd wonder, *why did Larry get to go?* He seemed happy there, living in a place that sounded so different from the chaos we were stuck in. But no one ever offered the same escape to me. I had to stay, forced to fend for myself in a house that felt like it was closing in on me every day.

Later, as I got older, the reality became clear. My father wasn't the solution I'd imagined. He had his own demons, and the life Larry had in Las Vegas wasn't what it seemed from the outside. Sure, he was away from the dysfunction we dealt with, but he was just trading one form of instability for another. I began to realize that if I had gone, I might've had it even worse there. My dad wasn't equipped to be a parent any more than my mom was.

Chapter Two: Beneath the Surface

By the time I reached high school, I was a ball of rage—angry at the world, angry at my family, angry at the life I had been given. It felt like I had been dealt the worst possible hand, one that I never asked for. I had been passed around, mistreated, and abused. I kept asking myself, *how much more was I supposed to endure?* I was drowning in pain, anger, and confusion, and I couldn't see a way out. Life felt like an endless cycle of hurt and disappointment. I didn't want to live anymore because, in my mind, there wasn't anything worth living for.

For years, I had put my mother on a pedestal, believing that she could do no wrong, even though she consistently made choices that hurt me. I justified her actions because she was my mother, and that title had always meant something. But by the time I hit high school, that blind loyalty was gone. I couldn't stand the sight of her anymore. I didn't want her to acknowledge me, and the few times she did, it was as if she was looking through me rather than at me. Her absence, which had always been a part of my life, became unbearable, even though our family had shrunk to just the three of us—me, her, and my younger sister, Toshianna. We had moved into a smaller house, but it felt like the walls were closing in on me. Trapped with my anger and resentment, I felt suffocated by the weight of it all.

By then, Toshi was in middle school, and with our mom still hardly around, I had to take on the responsibility of caring for her. It was my job to make sure she got on and off the bus, that she had food to eat, and that she was safe. But it was an impossible task. Toshi was unpredictable—she would have these wild outbursts, running outside in the dead of winter without a coat or shoes, or darting across the street without looking. I had to keep my eyes on her constantly, never able to relax. I wasn't just her sister; I had to be her caretaker, protector, and guardian.

Getting Toshi to school every day became more than just a routine—it was a survival tactic. School meant food, and that was one less meal I had to figure out how to provide. I started pocketing food from the cafeteria, saving it for later or for the weekend. On some days, I'd take Toshi with me to a friend's house, knowing that their parents would offer us dinner. That was another strategy for survival, making sure we had enough to get through the day.

But the burden of it all—caring for my sister, grappling with my mom's absence, feeling abandoned by the rest of my family—was unbearable. I wasn't just mad at my mom anymore. I was mad at every single one of my siblings, especially the older ones who had left me behind.

How could they just leave me like that? How could they escape, find their way out, and not even try to take me with them?

I felt completely abandoned. The only one I could bring myself to give grace to was Lamar. He had joined the military, trying to make something of his life, and at least he kept in touch. He would send letters, call, email—he always found a way to reach out to me, no matter where I was. But the rest of them? They seemed just as guilty as my mom in my eyes.

One day, I had reached my breaking point. The weight of my anger was too heavy to bear, and I needed answers. I called Trish, ready to unload all the fury I had been carrying. I gripped the phone so tightly my knuckles turned white. The anger I'd been carrying for years surfaced as soon as Trish picked up.

"Why didn't you ever come for me?" I demanded, my voice shaking. "Why didn't you take me with you? Did you even care about me at all?"

There was a pause on the other end, a deep breath, and then she said softly, "You don't know everything."

"What's that supposed to mean?" I shot back. "I was a kid, Trish. You left me there. She left me there."

"I didn't leave you," she replied, her voice steady but sad. "I was left too."

I froze, not expecting that.

"You were left?" I repeated, confused.

"Yeah," she continued. "You think the first time Mom abandoned anyone was when she left you at Grandma's? You don't know the half of it. I was 14, pregnant, and she told me she'd be gone for the weekend. Asked me to watch you and the boys while she went to Minnesota."

I was silent, processing her words.

"She didn't come back for six months," Trish said quietly. "Six. Months. I was a kid myself, pregnant, trying to take care of you all. And when she finally did come back, ready to move to Minnesota for good… there wasn't enough room in the car for me."

"What?" I whispered, my heart sinking.

"She left me behind," Trish said, her voice cracking. "Just like she left you."

My anger evaporated, replaced by shock. All this time, I thought I had been the only one she abandoned, but I wasn't alone in that pain.

I was devastated. All the anger I had toward Trish melted into something else—guilt, sorrow, and empathy. I had been so angry at her, thinking she had abandoned me, but now I realized she had been abandoned, too. She had been a child, just like me, and our mother had left her to fend for herself. I couldn't imagine the pain she must have felt, and suddenly, my anger toward her felt misplaced. I felt horrible for blaming her when she had been just as much a victim as I was.

But that conversation sparked a curiosity in me. It made me realize that I needed more answers. There were so many pieces of our family's story that didn't make sense, and I needed to understand why things had turned out the way they did. I decided to reach out to Diane, hoping that she could help me make sense of everything. Maybe she had the answers I was looking for. Maybe she could help me finally understand the truth behind the chaos that had defined my life.

For months, I tried every avenue I could think of to reach Diane—calling old numbers, asking relatives, even looking her up online—but it was like she had vanished. Every time I asked my mom about her, the conversation took a sharp turn. My mom's usual short temper exploded into full-blown fury at the mere mention of Diane's name. She would scream that she didn't want to talk about it, and that Diane had crossed a line so severe that they would never speak again. I couldn't fathom what could have caused such a rift. My mom had always been quick to anger, but this was different—her rage ran deep, as if it had festered for years.

It made me wonder: *What would Diane have possibly done to make my mother so furious? Had Diane been the catalyst for the bitterness and dysfunction that had ruled our family for as long as I could remember?*

Maybe whatever happened with Diane was the key to understanding my mom, the key to unlocking why she was the way she was.

I replayed countless scenarios in my head, trying to guess what could have happened.

Did Diane betray her in some unimaginable way?

It gnawed at me because if I could figure out why my mom was so angry with Diane, maybe I could finally understand why she had been so hard and distant with all of us.

After months of fruitless attempts, I finally managed to get Diane on the phone. We didn't have much of a relationship, in fact, we have probably only spoken a few times in my life. The moment I heard her voice, I could tell something was wrong.

Me: "Hey, Diane... it's been a while."

Diane: *[sighs]* "Yeah, it has. How are you?"

There was something in her voice. A heaviness I hadn't expected, and for a second, I froze. I knew I had to ask her, and had to confront what had torn everything apart, but instead, the words just got stuck in my throat.

Me: "I'm... I'm good. Just, you know, same old stuff. How about you?"

Diane: *[pauses]* "I've been better."

Her answer was short, almost clipped. She wasn't giving much away, but I could feel it— something was wrong. This was my chance. The moment I had been building up to for months. But I chickened out. There was something in the tone of her voice, a thickness that hinted at battles she was already fighting.

Me: "Yeah, I know how it is... uh, how's everything going over there with work and the kids?"

I was scrambling, trying to steer the conversation anywhere but toward the reason I called.

Diane: "it's going. Just trying to make it through each day, I guess."

Her voice was flat, emotionless. I could sense she really didn't feel like talking or being asked questions, but instead of pushing, I took the easy way out.

Me: "I hear you. We all are, right? Anyway, I'm glad I got to hear your voice. We should do this more often."

Diane: "Yeah, we should."

There was a long pause. It felt like the silence was begging me to say something more, to dig deeper. But I didn't. Her voice sounded like she was carrying more than she could bear, and I didn't want to add a very uncomfortable conversation to the mix of what she was already potentially dealing with.

Me: "Well, take care, okay? Let's stay in touch."

Diane: "I will. Take care."

The call ended with the same emptiness it started with. I had let the moment slip by, avoiding the real conversation. The one that had been festering beneath the surface for so long. The unresolved tension lingered, the weight of it still pressing down on me as I stared at the phone in my hand.

After that phone call, my sleep became restless. I started having disturbing dreams where Diane was pregnant, and my mother was screaming at her, pointing an accusing finger as Diane stood silently, her eyes wide with fear. The dreams were so vivid that they clung to me during the day while I was awake, haunting me with images I couldn't shake. The more I tried to push them aside, the more persistent they became.

One day, sitting in math class at Edison High School, I found myself drifting into a flashback. It was winter, and my mom and I were trudging through the snow to catch the bus near Merwin Liquor store. I was small, whining about the cold, dragging my feet as my mom pulled me along, urging me to hurry up. The scene felt so real, like I was back in that moment. But then, in the middle of the memory, something shifted. My mom, who had been hurrying me along, suddenly stopped and turned to me, her face serious. "Your dad had a baby with your sister!" she snapped.

The words hit me like a punch in the gut. My body reacted before my mind could catch up—I shot up from my seat in class and bolted to the bathroom, my heart raced. I stood in front of the mirror, my hands gripped the sink as I tried to steady myself. My head was spinning, my breath came in short, panicked bursts.

How could I have thought such a thing?

The idea was grotesque, horrifying. I splashed water on my face, trying to shake off the terrible thought, but it clung to me, making my stomach churn.

For the rest of the day, I tried to push the thought away, but it followed me like a shadow. A few days later, I couldn't stand it anymore. I found my mom in the kitchen, busy with something at the counter. My stomach twisted as I approached, but I had to ask.

"Mom," I started, my voice tight. "I need to ask you something."

She didn't turn around, but I could see her shoulders tense.

"What girl?" she replied, her tone neutral, almost too casual.

I swallowed hard. "Is it true? Did Dad... did he have a kid with Diane?"

She froze, the silence filling the room like a thick fog. My heart pounded in my chest, expecting her to laugh it off, to say I was crazy for even thinking that.

But instead, she just stood there, not saying a word.

The silence stretched on, unbearable.

"Mom?" I pressed, my voice shaking. "Did he?"

Finally, she turned around, her face blank, unreadable. For a moment, she just looked at me, and then, almost too quietly to hear, she said, "Yea, now leave me alone."

I felt like the ground had been ripped from beneath me.

The truth came out in jagged fragments, each one worse than the last. There had been signs—evidence—of my father's sexual abuse toward Diane, things that should have been obvious, glaring red flags that couldn't be ignored. It started when she was just 8 years old and she gave birth to their first child at 18.

Child Protective Services had been involved at some point, but even then, my mom let him come back. I couldn't wrap my mind around it.

Why would she let him return? Why didn't she protect Diane?

Trish shared the details with me when I was older, believing I would be better equipped to understand them. She told me that my father moved to Nevada to find a house for us, and my mom had instructed him to take Diane with him. I couldn't believe what I was hearing. My mom had sent Diane—her child, my sister—with a man she knew was dangerous. It was incomprehensible. My father found a house, set everything up for us to join him, but at the last minute, my mom made a decision. She told him, "We're not coming." Just like that, she left Diane with him.

I could hardly breathe as she told me this. I felt sick, not just with anger but with betrayal.

How could my mother, the person who was supposed to protect us, do something like this? How could she choose to send Diane into harm's way, knowing what she knew? And now, after everything, she had the nerve to be angry at Diane?

The more I thought about it, the more I realized the absurdity of it all. Diane had been the victim, not the villain. Yet, my mom had twisted the story in her mind, making Diane the one to blame.

This revelation shattered me. It crushed whatever remaining illusions I had about my mother's role in my life. I had always known she was flawed—angry, volatile, distant—but this was different. This was a betrayal so deep that it felt like it had cracked something inside me that could never be repaired.

This dark family secret explained so much about Diane's pain and distance. It added layers to the already complex emotions I had towards my mother and our family dynamics. Knowing that my mother had failed to protect Diane in such a profound way made it harder to reconcile with her actions and the choices she made.

Diane stayed with my father. I tried to make sense of it.

How could she stay with a man who had hurt her so deeply, both physically and emotionally?

But then, over time, the picture became even more complicated. She didn't just stay—she had four more children with him. Four! I struggled to understand it. Was it love? Was it fear? Or maybe it was something darker, something that kept her bound to him in ways that defied reason.

Stockholm syndrome, they call it. It's when the victim begins to identify with their captor, to sympathize with them despite the abuse they've suffered. At the time, I didn't have a name for it, but looking back, I wonder if that's what happened to my sister. It was like she couldn't break free, as if the trauma had rewired her thinking. She stayed with him, bore more of his children, and continued to live in this warped cycle where the boundaries between love and control were blurred beyond recognition.

Maybe it was the manipulation, or the isolation, or the fact that he was the father of her children. I'll never know for sure.

Diane's decisions puzzled me for years. It's as if she tried to rationalize what couldn't be rationalized—she clung to him, as if he was the only thing that made sense in a world that had stopped making sense a long time ago. Even as my siblings and I grew up, we could never fully understand the reasons behind her choices. All we could see was the damage, the unhealed wounds that never seemed to close.

Before I even realize it, tears are falling down my face. Hot streaks of emotion spilling over, the strength I have been holding onto for so long slowly evaporates. I quickly wipe them away, hurriedly swiping at my face with the back of my hand, desperate to erase any trace of them before anyone can notice. It isn't that I don't want to cry—it is that I can't afford to. Not now, not here.

The cool air in the hospital room kisses my wet cheeks, the moisture from my tears catching the sterile chill of the room, creating an odd sensation—like a fan is blowing directly on me. It sends a shiver through me, a physical reminder of the cold, unfeeling space I was in. I look over at my mother, still sleeping, still peaceful.

I have learned to hide my tears well over the years. It is a skill I developed out of necessity, something I have mastered from a young age. There is no room for tears in the world I have grown up in. No room for vulnerability. It is easier to pretend that everything is fine than to let anyone see the cracks in my armor. But in this moment, in this cold hospital room, with my mother laying ill and the weight of everything crashing down on me, the tears come anyway.

They are silent but heavy. Each drop feels like it is carrying years of pain, confusion, and exhaustion. The kind of tears that fall without warning, as if your body is finally rebelling against the facade you've been maintaining for far too long.

I turn my face slightly, hoping the dim lighting in the room will keep my tears invisible, but the wetness makes my cheeks glisten. I keep wiping them, determined to control what feels uncontrollable. I cannot break down now. Not when there is so much for me to hold together. But as I sit here, I can't help but feel the overwhelming sense of isolation. The coolness on my face only heightens it, a stark contrast to the burning ache in my chest.

I never told my mom about the abuse I endured at the hands of her boyfriend's brother. I often wonder whether she would have cared if I had. There were definitely signs that something was wrong, signs that any mother should have noticed. *But did she?*

I remember the desperation in my voice when I'd cry and beg her not to leave me at his house. My little hands clutching at her, hoping to hold her in place long enough to change her mind. But no matter how much I pleaded, it didn't matter. I told her they were mean to me—his wife, his kids—they'd say things that stung in ways I couldn't yet understand, but I thought that would be enough. I thought she'd hear the pain in my voice, see the fear in my eyes. But it wasn't.

I still don't know why it wasn't.

I'd watch her leave, feeling the walls close in on me. The pit in my stomach would grow heavier with each step she took toward the door. And then it would be just me. Me and him.

He had a wife, kids of his own, but none of that stopped him. I couldn't understand how no one else could see it, how no one else noticed the way he watched me. His eyes followed me as I walked, as I played outside, like a predator stalking prey. It wasn't loud or obvious, but it was there—unspoken, but unmistakable.

Why didn't anyone see it?

His wife—did she know? She had to have seen something, right?

Women know when something's off in their own home. But maybe she didn't want to. Maybe she drowned it out in the alcohol that was always flowing in that house. They were heavy drinkers, all of them, and maybe the haze of liquor blurred the lines of what was right and wrong. Maybe it kept the truth hidden, pulling a veil over their eyes.

Or maybe she just didn't want to know.

I used to hear stories about him. Whispers of his promiscuity, of the women he fooled around with. But never children. No one ever mentioned children. It was always adults, other women, messy affairs. But deep down, I knew. I knew that what I was experiencing was different. I just didn't have the words for it then, the vocabulary to explain what was happening.

Looking back, I wonder if everyone just chose not to see it. They drank their way through life, laughed through the haze of alcohol and secrets, leaving people like me—small, scared, voiceless—at the mercy of men like him.

I vividly recall a day when I was around ten years old. It was during one of our backyard barbecues—a rare moment when my mom's friends gathered, their children running around, the scent of grilled food filling the air. On the surface, everything seemed perfect. Laughter, music, the crackling of charcoal—it was almost easy to forget the tension I carried with me. At one point, I asked my mom if I could ride my bike. She agreed, but there was a catch: I had to get it from the basement myself.

I remember my heart sinking at her words. The basement. My stomach tightened as I thought about that dark, cold space. The fear washed over me, and I tried to swallow it back.

"Do I have to?" I asked quietly, hoping she'd change her mind.

"Yes, now go before I change my mind," she said, waving her hand dismissively.

I hesitated, staring at the door that led to the basement. I didn't know how to explain why I couldn't do it. I was terrified of the dark, of the shadows that seemed to stretch out in every corner down there. But how could I tell her that without sounding ridiculous?

"Please," I whispered, trying one last time. "Can't you get it for me?"

But she didn't budge, and I knew I had no choice. I stood there for a moment longer, gathering my courage, before slowly stepping toward the basement door, feeling the weight of my fear in every step.

Then, he offered to help. The moment he spoke, my stomach twisted into knots. By this time, the abuse had been going on for a couple of years, and I knew what his "help" meant.

"Never mind. I don't want my bike anymore," I quickly said, hoping that would end it.

But my mom, not understanding—or maybe not caring—became angry. She accused me of being rude, snapping, "Let him help you!"

Despite my protests, despite the tears welling up in my eyes, she pushed me to go with him.

Reluctantly, I followed him to the basement, but the weight of dread hung over me like a cloud. We were down there for much longer than it would have taken to simply grab my bike.

Did she not notice how much time had passed? Did she not wonder where we were? Or, more hauntingly, did she already know what was happening and choose to ignore it? Would she have been angry with me if I had brought it up?

It seems absurd to ask if my mom knew about the abuse, but the truth is, my mother wasn't entirely innocent in the way she handled things. There were darker layers to her life, secrets I didn't fully understand until much later.

All my life, we believed my mom's long-term boyfriend was my little sister's father. But when I was 14, that belief was shattered. A big fight erupted between my mom and her best friend. The shouting match between them echoed through the house, the walls practically vibrating from the tension. I sat on the stairs, trying to stay out of sight, but the words were impossible to ignore.

"I can't believe you, Ann!" her best friend screamed, her voice cracking with a mix of disbelief and fury. "After everything...this doesn't add up! None of it does!"

My mom's voice, sharp and defensive, fired back. "What are you talking about? Girl, get out of my face!"

"Or what?!" Her friend wasn't backing down. "You expect me to believe all this, that he's not her father, and nothing's off? You know damn well this don't add up!"

My heart pounded in my chest. I wasn't exactly sure what they were talking about, but I could feel it. Something big was unraveling. I wanted to ask, to demand answers, but I knew better. My mom's voice replayed in my head: *"Stay in a child's place."*

I leaned in, catching more of the argument.

"How could you lie about something like this? Does he even know?

My mom hesitated, and that pause said more than her next words. "You don't understand...this isn't your business."

"Not my business? That's my son! We are getting a damn DNA test! I can't believe you would do this—to her, to him, to everyone!"

I froze. DNA test? I didn't understand the full scope of it, but I knew enough to know that this wasn't the usual chaos that I was used to. Something was different this time. I didn't move, didn't breathe, hoping that if I stayed quiet enough, invisible enough, I might catch a glimpse of the truth before I was told to "stay in a child's place" again.

My mom's best friend lowered her voice, though it was still seething with anger. "You know this isn't right. You need to fix this, Ann. This is going to blow up in your face."

"Get out," my mom hissed. "Get out of my muthafucking house!"

Silence followed, heavy and uncomfortable. I stayed frozen on the steps as her best friend stormed out, slamming the door behind her.

I didn't ask questions that night, just tucked the conversation away, trying to put together the pieces I had overheard.

Months passed by and the argument between my mom and her best friend lingered, putting a wedge in their friendship and causing tension in our home.

The day started off with a heaviness that clung to the air, though I couldn't quite put my finger on why. My mom had told us earlier that we were going to her friend's house for a get-together, and I thought it would be like all the other gatherings they had—laughter, music, BBQ, and familiar faces. But something felt different as we pulled up.

When we arrived, the yard was packed with cars, far more than usual. I noticed new faces mixed in with the regulars, but there wasn't the usual upbeat vibe. No music thumped from the speakers, and instead of laughter, there was a low murmur of chatter that felt...off.

After stepping inside to say my hellos, I could feel the weight of the room. The energy was tense, like everyone was holding their breath, waiting for something. My mom gave me a nudge and told me, "Go outside and play with the kids." Her voice was even, but I could tell she was anxious about something. I didn't question it and headed out, trying to push the unease out of my mind.

Outside, I joined the other kids, but even the usual games felt flat. The sound of muted conversations from inside drifted through the windows, and although I couldn't make out the words, I knew something was happening. My instincts were screaming that this wasn't just another BBQ.

Then, it happened. The yelling.

At first, it was muffled, like someone was trying to keep their voice down, but soon it escalated. The shouts cut through the air, making all the kids stop in our tracks. I strained to hear what was going on, but I couldn't make out much. I caught bits and pieces—my mom's voice rising and then another woman, sharp and furious.

I peeked through the window, my heart pounding. Inside, my mom stood, face flushed with anger, locked in a heated argument with her best friend. Others stood around them, some trying to intervene, others just watching, stunned.

"I can't believe you!" Her friend shouted, "None of this adds up! You lied to me!"

I tried not to listen, but the voices grew louder.

My mom's friend was pacing, her fist balled up. "After all these years? How could you?!"

The yelling escalated. My mom's voice cut through the air. "I didn't plan for this shit to happen! But why are you acting like you didn't know we were fucking! Don't stunt for the rest of these muthafuckas. You knew!"

Her friend shot back. "Bitch he was a kid! You knew better!"

The DNA results had come back.

It wasn't until later that I pieced it all together— the whispers, the math, the truth that sent shockwaves through our family. My little sister's father wasn't my mom's long-term boyfriend like we'd always believed. It was her best friend's son ! At first, that alone didn't seem too strange, but as I began to calculate the years, the weight of it hit me.

My mom was 50 years old now, and her best friend's son was 27. But my sister was 11, which meant that when she was born, my mom was 39 and he was just 16.

Sixteen!!

The realization crashed over me like a tidal wave, sweeping away everything I thought I knew. My mother had a child with a teenager, a boy. The questions flooded my mind, racing faster than I could process.

How could she do that? Why didn't I know? What did this mean about who my mother really was?

I stood outside that house, the sun bright overhead, but all I could feel was the cold sinking in my gut.

After this revelation I began struggling significantly with my relationship with God. What hurt the most was the spiritual disillusionment. If there really was a God, why did He let all of this happen? Why would a loving, all-powerful being stand by while we suffered—homeless, hungry, broken? Wasn't He supposed to protect us, provide for us, love us? The more I thought about it, the angrier I became. Believing in God felt like falling for the same empty promises my mother clung to—a desperate hope that led nowhere.

As I grew older, the bitterness hardened into skepticism. I built walls around my heart, determined never to be fooled by faith or manipulated by religion. God became a distant concept, a figure I couldn't trust or rely on. In my mind, He was either indifferent or nonexistent, and either way, He wasn't there for us when we needed Him the most.

A lot to take in huh? Heavy stuff right? Well, this is only the beginning so pay attention.

Chapter Three: Shattered Trust, Fragile Lies

My mom's awake now, in pain, and growing more irritable by the second. Her mood swings have become almost predictable.

"Where's my chicken?" she demands, her voice raspy but still sharp.

It's one of the few things that brings her comfort these days—fried chicken from Popeyes. In these moments, I've learned to use it as a tool to coax her into following the treatment plan.

"After your physical therapy session," I reply gently, knowing the promise of chicken will keep her calm for now.

I rush to the bathroom, my mind still buzzing with the weight of my memories. When I return, it's time to help her get ready for therapy. Every movement is slow and deliberate as I dress her, each task a stark reminder of how far we've come and how much has changed. Most days my mom would reject help from the nurses in any and every way. The only way we could get her to cooperate is if I was there helping. As her health began to decline she looked for me to have the answers to all of her questions and worries. Any time the doctor wanted to change a medication or treatment plan she would say, "call my daughter". Once she's settled into her wheelchair, I watch the nurse take her away.

A sense of relief washes over me as I check the time. There's a brief window for me to step out and check on my kids. Balancing my role as a mother and a caretaker feels like a never-ending juggling act. Both need me, but in different ways. The weight of responsibility is immense, yet I can't let either fall. I've made it this far—there's no turning back now.

As I step outside, the cool air hits my face, and I pause for a moment to breathe. The fresh air feels like a small victory, a reminder that even amidst the chaos, there are moments of quiet. But the quiet doesn't last long. I'm four months pregnant, and the exhaustion is catching up with me. My body aches, and my mind is constantly racing, thinking about what needs to be done, who needs my attention, what fires I need to put out next.

But for now, I have this brief moment to myself before the whirlwind begins again.

I get into my car and sit there for a few minutes, letting the silence wash over me. The exhaustion runs deep in my bones, a familiar ache that never seems to fully go away. As I sit there, suspended between the present and the weight of everything I've been through, my mind starts to drift back to my younger years—before life became the complex web of responsibilities it is today.

I remembered the first time I was pregnant at 17, I found myself completely overwhelmed by my circumstances. I dropped out of high school, unsure of what my future held. I didn't see myself as special or capable of achieving much, but I clung to the hope that this baby—my baby—would love me unconditionally. I believed that she would fill the void I had carried with me for as long as I could remember. I moved in with Jay, my child's father, a decision driven more by necessity than love, and began navigating life without any guidance or clear direction.

Jay and I met when I was 15, just shy of turning 16. His house became my sanctuary, an escape from the emptiness of my own home. His mother worked nights and slept most of the day, so no one was ever really around, which made it easy for me to retreat there. At my house, it was just me. My mother was gone for longer stretches now that I was "almost grown," as she'd say. My baby sister was usually with her, and my older siblings had all moved out. I felt like a ghost in my own home.

Being with Jay gave me something I craved—a sense of normalcy, however fleeting. I wasn't just floating through life when I was with him; I had a place to go, someone to be with. But while I found solace in his presence, I realized that normalcy wasn't enough. What I truly needed was support.

The support I needed came from the most unexpected source—a relentless and, at times, annoying school counselor named Becky Koltes. She saw something in me that I couldn't see in myself. No matter how much I resisted her efforts, she wouldn't give up. She was persistent in her belief that I could finish school, and it was her relentless encouragement that eventually pushed me to return. I enrolled in an alternative school tailored for teen mothers, and it was there that I truly began to change.

Becky became more than a counselor; she was a lifeline. She cared for me in a way that no one ever had, not out of pity, but with genuine, selfless concern. She saw through my pain, my anger, and my self-destructive behaviors, and she wouldn't let me spiral out of control. Whenever I had an excuse not to show up, she had a solution.

One afternoon, I sat slumped in Becky's office, staring at the worn carpet. She waited patiently, as always, giving me the silence I needed to pull myself together. Finally, she spoke.

"You're here today," she said softly, her eyes warm with that same steady, unflinching kindness that never seemed to fade. "I'm glad."

I scoffed, trying to brush off the significance of it. "I almost didn't come. Missed the bus," I mumbled, half hoping she'd let me off the hook, that maybe she'd finally give up on me.

Becky tilted her head, eyebrows raised. "And I'm sure if I hadn't sent that cab, you'd be off doing something that'd land you in even more trouble, right?"

I didn't answer, but a faint grin tugged at my lips. Somehow, she always knew. She knew me in a way that no one ever had.

"Why do you care so much?" I blurted, finally meeting her eyes. "I mean… What's in this for you? I'm not your problem."

Her face softened, and she leaned forward, hands folded. "It's simple. I care because you're worth it. Not because of what you've been through or what you've done. You, just as you are, matter."

I looked away, her words sinking in like stones, heavy and unfamiliar. "No one's ever… said that to me before," I whispered.

She reached across the table and placed her hand gently on mine. "You're not alone anymore. I'll be here, even on the days you don't want to show up. And I'll keep believing in you, even when you can't."

I swallowed, her words settling into some deep, forgotten part of me.

"Becky, what if I'm just… too messed up to fix?"

She smiled, that same patient smile that somehow gave me strength. "I don't believe anyone's beyond repair. Besides," she added with a small laugh, "you're not a project. You're

53

a person. And I'm just here to help you see what I already see—a future beyond all this."

For the first time, a flicker of something like hope stirred within me. "You really think… I could have a different life?"

She nodded, her gaze unwavering. "Absolutely. It starts with believing that you're worth it."

She taught me how to communicate, how to trust that not everyone was out to hurt me. Slowly, I began to realize that my life didn't have to be a product of my environment. There was more to me than the circumstances I was born into. For the first time, I began to envision a future beyond the chaos of my present, and it was because of her that I held onto hope. But hope alone wasn't enough to anchor me to the relationship Jay and I had.

We stayed together until my daughter turned one. There were no major issues between us—no cheating, no drama. I think we just drifted apart. I was searching for something different, although at the time, I didn't even know what "different" meant. Looking back, I think I was bored. I was still so young, an immature teenager trying to navigate adulthood without a map. I had no clue what was truly good for me.

Not long after our breakup, I found myself back in the dating scene, still trying to figure out what I wanted. A friend introduced me to a guy named Sam. He was nine years older than me, and everything about him screamed excitement. He was so fine, had money, and drove nice cars. He exuded confidence and charm, and I fell for it instantly. He snatched me up so quickly, and I let him because I thought he had everything I needed. I didn't realize then that I was chasing an illusion, mistaking material things for stability and security.

What started as a promising relationship quickly turned into a trap. Trying to move forward and finish school felt impossible with the weight of my new relationship holding me down. I had dreams—ones that felt just out of reach—but with him there, they started to seem ridiculous. He was older, controlling, and relentless, and he made sure I knew I couldn't live without him. Every time I tried to leave, he pulled me back, his threats filling me with dread.

I found some safety with Becky, my counselor, who had become a source of comfort in my life.

But even with her, I couldn't bring myself to share the darkest parts. I kept quiet about him, afraid of what he might do if he found out I was reaching out for help. Every time I thought about telling Becky, I'd see his face in my mind—cold, angry, and calculating. He knew how to manipulate me, using fear like a weapon, and my silence kept me bound to him.

Sam always found ways to make sure I felt trapped. He would remind me constantly, "You're nothing without me. No one else would put up with you and your baggage." He'd drop veiled threats, whispering that he could make me disappear or hurt my baby if I ever tried to leave him. I knew what he was capable of; I'd seen his anger, felt his power over me. I started to believe him, convincing myself there was no safe way out.

It became my new normal—this life of isolation and silence, where fear was my constant companion. I felt like I was drowning, caught between wanting a future and being too afraid to reach for it.

Then one day, I reached my breaking point. I told him I was leaving town, cut off contact with everyone who might give me away, and went into hiding. I stayed locked inside my house, only leaving to attend school. Only my best friend and one other person, Tee, knew the truth of my plan. Tee was also a good friend of Sam, but I trusted him because he used to always tell me that I needed to get out of that situation. Tee and I had a secret friendship, one I maintained for months, filled with anxiety and constant vigilance.

Sam would never have been okay with Tee and I being friends—or with me having any relationship with any man that wasn't blood related. His jealousy wasn't just intense; it was suffocating. It didn't matter if the connection was platonic or professional; in his eyes, any man was a threat to his control over me. Tee, with his genuine concern and easygoing nature, was no exception.

It was a quiet morning, the kind where you almost forget the danger that lurks in the corners of your life. I thought I was safe. The house was still, and my sister had just shouted her usual goodbye as she rushed out the door for school.

"Bye! See you later sister!" she yelled, the sound of her voice fading as she left.

I let out a small breath of relief. The day was starting off normal, and maybe, just maybe, I could relax a little, at least for a while. But then, minutes later, the front door creaked open again. Confused, I called out, thinking she must've missed the bus.

"Did you forget something?" I shouted, hoping to hear her voice.

But instead of the light, hurried footsteps of my sister, I heard something heavier. Thudding. My stomach twisted as I listened to the sound of shoes that sounded way too big to belong to my sister slowly thudding up the stairs, growing louder with each step. I froze.

Suddenly, his voice cut through the silence like a blade.

"So, you've been lying?"

My heart plummeted into my stomach. That voice—it was him, Sam. Without thinking, I grabbed my baby, holding her close, my hands trembling as I ran for the closet. I tucked her inside, pulling the door closed just as I heard his footsteps stop right outside my room.

I pressed myself against the wall, trying to steady my breathing, but it was no use. The door burst open, and there he was. His eyes were wild, filled with fury. He was bigger than I remembered, or maybe it was the fear making him seem that way. He towered over me, and before I could even say a word, he lunged.

His hands wrapped around my neck like a vice-grip, squeezing harder and harder. I clawed at him, kicking, trying to break free, but it was no use. He was stronger, too strong. I felt the air being stolen from my lungs, my vision started to blur.

Is this it? Is this how I die?

In my last desperate effort, I gasped out words I didn't even think about.

"I'm sorry! I'm sorry!" I choked. "I love you…"

The words felt like acid on my tongue, but somehow, they reached him. His grip loosened just enough for me to gulp down a breath. He stared at me for a moment, eyes dark and unreadable, before letting go completely. He stormed out of the room, leaving me crumpled on the floor, gasping for air, tears streaming down my face.

I lay there, shaking, my hand clutching my throat, struggling to pull myself together. I could hear the sound of his footsteps fade as he left the house. For a moment, all I could hear was my heartbeat pounding in my ears, thudding as if it, too, was trying to recover from what had just happened.

I stumbled to the closet and opened the door. My baby was still there and safe. I cradled her close as my body trembled uncontrollably.

I don't know how he found me or figured out my, not so secret, hiding place. Tee and my best friend were the only ones aware of my plan. The plan was as desperate as it was necessary. I had to hide in plain sight, vanishing without really going anywhere. Sam had a way of always knowing where I was, of finding me no matter how much distance I tried to put between us. This time, I needed him to believe I was truly gone, out of town, far beyond his reach.

I had to stay home, turning my own space into a sanctuary of secrecy. I had no money or support system to actually go anywhere. I barely left the house, only for quick errands and going to school, because the risk of being seen was too great. I kept the curtains drawn tightly at all times, allowing no slivers of daylight to reveal movements inside. Every knock on the door, every sound outside, sent a shiver down my spine as I held my breath, praying it wasn't him. I hoped that eventually, he would stop looking, that his obsession would fizzle out once he believed I was truly gone. It wasn't a perfect plan, but it was all I had, and in that moment, survival depended on it.

The next day after my assault, I received a call informing me that Tee was in the hospital because Sam had stabbed him in the face. Now, with Tee attacked, I couldn't help but wonder—

Had Sam discovered the truth? Had he found out that Tee knew my real whereabouts, and was that why he was targeted?

I wasn't sure how much Sam had pieced together, but one thing was clear: I had to leave immediately. Tee's stabbing shook me to my core, underscoring the reality that nowhere was safe. The small circle of people who knew the truth was now compromised, and I realized that I had no place to go where I could truly be out of his reach. No one knew the full extent of my situation, and the few who did were too close to him or too vulnerable themselves. I felt cornered, my options shrinking by the minute, yet my desperation to escape only grew.

As I frantically started plotting my next move, Sam must have realized the gravity of what he had done to Tee. In a twisted attempt to smooth things over, he began reaching out to his associates to apologize, trying to repair the damage. But Tee wasn't having it—he refused to forgive him. This act of defiance from Tee was both comforting and terrifying. On one hand, I knew that Tee was loyal and would never betray me, he's proved that throughout our friendship. On the other hand, the more he stood up to Sam, the more danger he put himself in.

Despite everything, Tee reached out to check on me, asking how I was holding up and if I was safe. When I shared my growing concerns, he offered me a place to stay, assuring me that Sam would never come near him again after what had happened. I hesitated at first, concerned about the risk of Sam finding out, but I had nowhere else to turn. So, I took him up on his offer, hoping that being close to Tee would provide the safety and protection I so desperately needed.

Tee was vigilant, constantly checking in on me and making sure someone was with me at all times. He was my protector, even in the midst of his own reckless lifestyle. Though he lived on the edge, caught up in a world of danger and uncertainty, his care for me was genuine. He wanted better for me, and he often reminded me that I deserved more than the life I was trapped in. He believed in my potential, constantly encouraging me to return to high school. I had dropped out of school more than once, and now, at 19 years old with a one-year-old baby on my hip, the thought of going back felt overwhelming.

Despite being almost ten years older, I felt like Tee never saw me as just some naïve kid. He saw me as someone capable of breaking free from the life that seemed to define me, and his belief in me gave me a glimmer of hope.

At least that's what I thought.

Tee and I never had that deep connection most couples share—there wasn't love, and we certainly hadn't planned a future together. It felt more like a silent agreement than anything else. After all, he'd been there during some of the hardest times, helping me in ways no one else had, and I felt like I owed him for that. *But what could I give back?* It wasn't like I had anything tangible to offer. We spent so much time together, day after day, and eventually, things just…escalated. It wasn't about passion or romance, but more about familiarity, a need for comfort, maybe even a sense of obligation. And it kept happening, blurring lines that weren't meant to be crossed. Then, a few months later, reality hit me hard when I found out I was pregnant again, now with my second child.

I was terrified, but there was a flicker of hope that maybe this time things could be different. Part of me craved the idea of love and stability, even though I barely understood what that looked like or felt like. Love was a mystery to me, a vague idea I had picked up from movies or the rare glimpses of affection I'd seen in other people's lives.

What if this was it—my chance at a real connection, a fresh start—and I was too scared or too broken to see it for what it was?

A part of me held onto the belief that if I could make this work, maybe I'd finally find that sense of security and love I had always longed for. I wanted more than just a transactional relationship; I wanted a partner, someone to rely on. So I convinced myself that if I gave it my all, if I was patient, understanding, maybe, just maybe, we could build something real out of what felt like fragments. And so I stepped forward, holding onto hope that I could somehow mold our relationship into something lasting, something meaningful.

But just when I thought life couldn't get more complicated, tragedy struck again. My child's father, Tee, was in a devastating car accident that left him in a coma for twelve days.

During his hospital stay, I watched a steady stream of women come through those sterile, white corridors, each one holding a different piece of a life I hadn't known about. These weren't just friends; they were women he had been seeing—women he'd juggled while we were supposedly together. They weren't just showing up; they were calling constantly, sending money, bending over backward for him. It was like a painful puzzle unraveling before my eyes, and I was putting together pieces that didn't belong in the life I thought we shared.

Then I found out he had recently served time for pimping and pandering. By accident of course. I overheard a friend of his at the hospital bragging about "the fun times" they used to have. He was reliving stories that sounded like they were from a movie. It made me curious about his history so something inside me told me to look up his criminal history, and BOOM! Right on the internet in black and white. He was a pimp. The reality hit me like a cold shock, unraveling every feeling, every memory. Suddenly, nothing made sense.

Was any of it real? Had he cared at all, or had it all been part of some sick, manipulative plan?

I questioned my entire time with him, and then I questioned myself.

How could I have been so blind?

I was young and desperate for security, for someone to anchor me in the storm of my life. He had become that anchor. But now, it felt like that anchor had been yanked up, leaving me adrift and more broken than ever, questioning everything I thought I knew about loyalty, and about myself. Such a tragic incident happened and now I was questioning if this was a blessing in disguise.

How much would I have been willing to do for someone that I had felt saved me? Would I have been willing to be another one of those women selling their bodies?

His family didn't know me, and because of the series of events that happened with the stabbing and the accident, I was banned from the hospital, left to wonder whether he would live or die. Alone and pregnant, I turned once again to one of the only people I could trust: Becky.

Becky looked up as I walked into her office, her warm smile instantly easing some of the weight I'd been carrying.

"Hey, I'm so glad you're here. How are you doing?" she asked, her voice gentle but steady.

I shifted uncomfortably, feeling the urge to downplay everything, but she had this way of making me feel safe enough to be honest.

"I don't know," I finally admitted, my voice barely above a whisper. "Everything just feels…impossible. It's like I'm trying to get out of quicksand, but the more I try, the more I sink."

She nodded, understanding in her eyes. "It must feel overwhelming, but you've already come so far. Remember, you're not alone in this. You're so close to finishing school."

"School feels pointless sometimes," I said, looking down. "I mean, what's the use when everything else is falling apart?" I looked down as my eyes started to water.

Becky leaned forward, her voice low but firm. "You finishing school isn't just about academics—it's about giving yourself options. You've worked too hard to give up now. And it's okay if it feels hard, but don't let that take away from everything you've accomplished to get here."

"But… there's something I haven't told you." My voice wavered as I continued, "I'm pregnant again."

Becky's eyes softened as I sat there, broken open in front of her. She didn't flinch or look away.

"Congratulations", She said smiling.

I wiped a tear, embarrassed but also confused. "I just… I thought you'd be tired of me by now. Every time I come in here, it's more problems. More… messes."

She leaned forward, resting a hand on mine. "Hey," she said, her voice unwavering. "I'm not tired of you. You've been through so much more than anyone should ever have to go through. I'm here, okay?

Her words cut through my shame, offering a glimmer of hope.

With tears still streaming down my face, I managed a faint smile. For the first time, I felt like maybe I could make it through.

Months passed, then, out of the blue, the phone rang, and when I answered, his voice was hesitant.

"Hi, my name is Tee. I'm looking for Candice. Is this her?"

I frowned, caught off guard. His tone was unfamiliar, detached. "Tee? What's with the formal introduction? Why are you talking like that? And why are you just now calling me?"

There was a pause on the line, heavy and unsettling. "I don't know how to say this," he said quietly, almost apologetically. "I was in an accident. I don't remember you."

His words hit me like a punch to the gut. I gripped the phone tighter. "What do you mean you don't remember me? Tee, Stop playing."

"I know a little about you because I just got my phone back," he said, his voice steady but hollow. "I saw our messages. That's how I knew to call you. But…I don't remember anything about us or what we had. I'm sorry."

My heart dropped, and for a moment, I couldn't speak. This wasn't a joke. This wasn't some cruel prank. "So you're saying you don't remember anything? None of it?

"No," he admitted, his voice heavy with regret. "I wish I could, Candice. I really do. I've been trying to piece everything together, but it's all gone. The only reason I even know about the baby is because of the messages on my phone."

I felt tears sting my eyes, but I swallowed hard, refusing to let them fall. "This isn't fair," I whispered, more to myself than to him.

"I don't want to hurt you," he said, his voice soft but resolute. "I can't change what's happened. But I want to be here now. For the baby. For you, if you'll let me."

We talked for a few minutes more before he had to go, and as I hung up the phone, the reality of the situation began to set in. Tee wasn't the same person I had known before the accident.

All thoughts of us being together dissolved in that moment. His traumatic brain injury had changed him in many ways. I didn't know how to be there for him, how to support him through his healing journey. I wasn't equipped for this, and deep down, I knew I couldn't give him what he needed. Whatever future we had imagined for ourselves was gone, swept away in the cruel aftermath of his injury.

The accident had taken his memory, and along with it, any connection we once had. I was devastated, but by then, I was used to loss. A few weeks later, I gave birth to my second child alone. I graduated high school shortly after, but life didn't get easier.

Chapter Four: The Weight of Forgiveness

The years that followed were filled with more heartbreak, dead-end jobs, and failed relationships. I had 3 more children with different men, each time hoping it would be different, but it never was. The pain from my childhood, the neglect from my mother, haunted me and influenced every decision I made.

I told myself I would never be like her, but as much as I tried, I felt myself slipping into the same patterns. I struggled to provide for my children, just as she had struggled to provide for me. The weight of it all—the heartbreak, the failures, the unmet dreams—it crushed me. I blamed her for all of it. Look at what she did to me. Look at how she broke me.

I couldn't help but wonder if I would ever be able to escape the cycle. Or if I was destined to repeat it, no matter how hard I fought.

For some strange reason, my mom had a weird attachment to my kids. She was an active grandparent in a way I had never seen her be as a mother. She was present, nurturing, and attentive, almost as if she had been waiting her entire life for this role. She would coo over them, laugh with them, and spend hours just holding them in her arms. It was something beautiful to witness, but at the same time, it stung. I would sometimes get jealous because she was so good with them, so effortlessly maternal. I couldn't help but wonder—*why couldn't she be there for me like that? What has changed?* It was as if she had tapped into a reserve of love and care that I had never known existed when I was a child. This newfound connection with my kids left me feeling both grateful and deeply hurt, stirring up emotions I had long tried to bury.

Determined to provide a better future for my children and prove to myself that I could break the cycle, I decided to further my education. I enrolled in a program to become a Pharmacy Technician. It felt like a fresh start, a chance to finally build the stable life I had always dreamed of. During this time, my mom stepped in to watch the kids while I worked and attended classes. It was an arrangement that seemed almost too good to be true. For a while, everything was on the up and up.

I was finally becoming financially stable, something that had always seemed just out of reach. I got a better car, a bigger house for me and my kids, and a good-paying job. It felt like I was finally on solid ground, building the kind of life I had always wanted for my children—something far removed from the instability and chaos of my own upbringing. My mom being there to help felt like a missing piece of the puzzle finally falling into place.

But just when I thought things were finally falling into place, my mom threw me a curveball that I never saw coming. Without any heads-up or preparation, she decided she wanted to move to Mississippi. It wasn't a gradual decision or something we could plan around—she literally left that next weekend. I was blindsided. Her sudden departure left me scrambling and panicked, with no one to help with my kids.

Childcare was too expensive, and there was a two-year waiting list for childcare assistance. The walls of stability I had carefully built began to crumble around me. I couldn't make it to work with no babysitter, and without work, I couldn't pay the bills. It felt like the rug had been pulled out from under me. I lost everything

I had worked so hard to achieve. The car, the house, the job—they all slipped through my fingers like sand.

I felt like a failure. I didn't know what to do, where to turn. The weight of it all was crushing, and I was forced to make a decision that broke my heart. I had to do the one thing I promised I would never put my kids through. I went to a shelter. The irony was almost too much to bear. Once again, I found myself in the same suffocating cycle I had fought so hard to escape, one that had defined my childhood and now threatened to define my children's lives as well.

The shelter was a stark, unwelcome reminder of my childhood—a bitter echo of instability and uncertainty that seemed to press down on me as soon as I walked in. The air was thick, a mingling of smells that clung to everything: stale sweat, the sharp tang of bleach, and an underlying staleness that only places crowded with people and scant resources seem to have. Somewhere nearby, the sour scent of a recent diaper change lingered in the hall.

Babies wailed in uneven pitches, each cry winding its way down the narrow halls and into the corners, blending with the quiet murmur of mothers trying to hush or comfort them. Occasionally, a toddler's babbling or a child's laughter broke through the tension, creating a temporary warmth before fading back into the ambient noise.

My feet moved over the scratched linoleum floors as I carried my bags, careful not to brush against the walls where the paint had peeled and grime had settled into the cracks. Every sound was amplified—footsteps, the low hum of whispered conversations, the squeak of a door opening, and the dragging of heavy belongings being moved from one spot to another, as if anyone might leave at any moment.

It all came rushing back in a wave of painful nostalgia. But as much as it hurt to return to, the shelter also became a turning point. It was a place where I was forced to confront my reality head-on, to grapple with the challenges in front of me, and to reevaluate my priorities. There was no room for self-pity, only for action. It was a humbling experience that tested my resilience and determination in ways I never expected. Despite the immense setbacks and the emotional toll, I knew I had to find a way to rebuild, not just for the sake of my children but for myself as well. I couldn't let this be the end of our story.

During our 2-year shelter stay, I found myself in a place of both desperation and unexpected growth. The shelter wasn't just a roof over our heads; it became a place where I began to confront the deep-seated pain and trauma that had followed me for so long. I participated in groups like Forgiveness, Me, Myself, & Lies, and Boundaries—each session peeling back layers of hurt and revealing parts of myself that I had long kept buried. These groups were more than just meetings; they were lifelines, offering me tools to rebuild not just my life but my sense of self.

Forgiveness was a particularly challenging group for me. Sitting in a circle, surrounded by women with stories of their own, I realized that I had been carrying the weight of so much anger and resentment. The group taught me that forgiveness wasn't about excusing the wrongs done to me; it was about freeing myself from the burden of carrying them. I began to see that holding onto the pain only kept me tethered to the past, and if I wanted to truly move forward, I had to start letting go.

In Me, Myself, & Lies, I confronted the harsh, often destructive narratives I had told myself over the years. I had internalized so much of the negativity from my childhood, believing that I wasn't worthy of love or success, that I was destined to repeat the same cycles of failure. But through the guidance of the group, I began to rewrite those narratives, replacing them with affirmations of my strength, worth, and capability. It was a slow process, but each small shift in mindset became a stepping stone toward reclaiming my identity.

Boundaries was another crucial group that reshaped my approach to relationships. I had never really understood the concept of boundaries; my life had always been an open door, often at the expense of my own well-being. This group taught me that setting boundaries was not about keeping people out but about protecting my peace and ensuring that my relationships were healthy and reciprocal. It gave me the courage to start saying "no" without guilt and to prioritize my needs alongside those of my children.

My adult years were marked by resilience and a determination to break the cycle for my children. Despite the challenges, I continued to push forward, fueled by the desire to give my children a better life than the one I had. My journey through motherhood became a path of self-discovery, healing, and ultimately, a testament to the strength I inherited from my mother.

I know, right? I bet you're thinking, From your mother? What are you talking about? That lady was horrible to you.

It's easy to look at the surface and see only the pain and neglect, but the healing I went through after losing everything allowed me to see her as a person who was also trying to survive in her own flawed way. This realization didn't immediately heal our relationship, but it planted a seed of empathy that would later grow into a more profound understanding and forgiveness.

In the shelter, surrounded by other women who had their own stories of brokenness and survival, I began to unpack the layers of my mother's life. She wasn't just the woman who abandoned me or failed to provide stability— she was a person who had been through her own traumas, her own losses, her own battles. The same way I was fighting for my kids, she was fighting for us, even if her fight looked different. I started to recognize the weight of what she carried, the emotional and physical scars that shaped her decisions. She didn't always make the right choices, but who does when they're fighting just to stay afloat?

Through the groups at the shelter—Forgiveness, Me, Myself, & Lies, Boundaries—I began to see my mother in a different light. I learned that forgiveness isn't about erasing the past or pretending the pain didn't happen; it's about releasing the grip that pain has on your present. In those sessions, I found myself questioning the narratives I had held onto for so long—the ones that painted my mother as the villain in my story. It became clear that she wasn't just the antagonist in my life; she was a complex human being, shaped by circumstances that, as a child, I could never fully comprehend.

I recognized the strength it took for her to keep going, even when everything around her was falling apart. Yes, she made mistakes—many of them—but she also faced her own battles, battles I didn't fully understand until I started facing my own. My mother's life was marked by hardship, and while she may not have had the tools to cope in a way that protected her children, she did the best she could with what she had.

This shift in perspective didn't erase the hurt or the scars left by my childhood, but it did open the door to forgiveness—not just of my mother, but of myself. I forgave myself for the anger I had harbored, for the resentment that had eaten away at me for years. I forgave myself for the times I felt I had failed my own children, repeating some of the same mistakes I swore I'd never make. And in that forgiveness, I found a sense of peace that had long eluded me.

My journey wasn't just about breaking the cycle for my children; it was about breaking it for myself, too. In understanding my mother's struggles, I began to heal my own. I realized that strength isn't just about holding everything together perfectly—sometimes it's about surviving the mess and still finding the will to get up and try again. My mother's strength may not have looked like the kind I wanted or needed as a child, but it was strength nonetheless. And now, that same resilience runs through me, guiding me as I build a different life for my children, with the hope that they will one day understand my imperfections and forgive me, too.

Chapter Five: Fires of Change

As I began to reflect on my tumultuous childhood and the countless emotions it evoked, I started to piece together a different perspective—my mother's. For so long, I had seen her through the lens of my own pain, anger, and confusion. I had been a child who felt abandoned, neglected, and pushed aside, and that perspective shaped how I saw her for much of my life. But as I grew older and began to confront my own struggles, I realized that to truly understand her, I had to step outside of my hurt and look at her as more than just my mother. I had to see her as a woman with her own story, her own fears, and her own broken dreams.

My mother was a flawed woman, but she was also a product of her own hardships and experiences. She grew up in a time and place where survival was a daily battle, where being a single mother of seven children meant facing challenges that I couldn't fully comprehend as a child. Her life, her choices, and her faith were shaped by struggles I could only begin to understand.

My mother was shot in the head by her ex-husband in her earlier years. The physical trauma from that incident undoubtedly played a significant role in her irrational decision-making. I was stunned when I finally learned the truth about the shooting, a piece of family history that had always been shrouded in whispers and half-told stories. My older sister's father had a volatile temper and a habit of accusing my mother of infidelity. Those accusations, whether baseless or not, became a routine in their toxic relationship. But this particular argument escalated in a way none of us could have imagined.

It started with his suspicion about the paternity of their second child. He hurled accusations at her, his voice rising with anger and frustration. My mom, with her fiery personality, didn't back down. She argued right back, her words sharp and defiant. That was the thing about her—she was fearless, even in the face of danger. She didn't cower; she fought.

But he wasn't just angry. He wanted to scare her, to assert his control. That's when he pulled out the pistol. I imagine the air in the room must have shifted in that moment, thick with tension and fear. The weight of his actions settled on my mom, but instead of recoiling, she charged at him. She wasn't one to be intimidated, not even by a loaded weapon.

A short tussle ensued—a chaotic blur of movement and desperation. I pictured the room filled with the sound of grunts and shouted threats, and furniture scraping against the floor as they struggled. Then, the deafening crack of the gun going off.

The bullet found its mark, changing her life forever. As much as I know about the event, there are still parts of it that remain a mystery to me, details lost in the chaos of that day. What I do know is that my mother survived, with scars, both physical and emotional. That moment defined her in so many ways—her resilience, her recklessness, and her unyielding spirit. She wasn't afraid of anything, not even death, but that fearlessness came at a price.

The more I reflected, the more I realized that her actions, as irrational and reckless as they often seemed, were deeply rooted in her reality—a reality fraught with fear, scarcity, and a desperate need to believe in something greater than herself.

Adding to her burdens, The injury likely affected her cognitive abilities and emotional stability, making it even harder for her to navigate the challenges of life and motherhood. She was no longer the same woman she had been before the incident. The trauma didn't just impact her mind; it fractured her spirit, leaving her to navigate life with a mind that didn't always work as it should and a heart that had been shattered.

My mother's erratic behavior, her absences, and her inability to provide stability were rooted in a deep-seated struggle against an unforgiving world. She was fighting battles we couldn't understand, with weapons we couldn't see. Her decisions, though often detrimental, were her attempts to navigate a life filled with obstacles that seemed unconquerable.

As I began to reflect, I started to see the desperation behind her actions. She clung to faith as if it were her last lifeline, believing with every fiber of her being that God would provide, that He would somehow make a way out of no way. Her faith wasn't just a religious belief; it was her survival mechanism. She didn't have the luxury of rationality. She was in survival mode, doing whatever she could to keep her head above water, even if her choices seemed reckless to those of us on the outside.

I realized that my mother's lack of affection wasn't a reflection of her love for us but a symptom of her emotional struggles. Her past, her disappointments, and her battles with life, shaped her into a person who believed love was shown through endurance, not words or hugs.

As I pieced together these fragments of her life, I began to see her not as the villain of my story, but as a fellow survivor. Yes, she made mistakes—many of them—but those mistakes were born out of desperation to survive in a world that had been anything but kind to her. Understanding this didn't erase the pain of my childhood, but it did give me a new perspective. It allowed me to see her as a person, flawed and fragile, just like me. And in that understanding, I found a measure of compassion that I never thought I could feel.

It didn't make everything okay, but it did make it a little easier to carry the weight of our shared past. My anger transformed into a complex mix of sadness, understanding, and forgiveness. My mother's life was a tapestry of mistakes and misguided decisions, but it was also a testament to her resilience and unyielding faith. In understanding her perspective, I began to heal and find compassion for the woman who, despite everything, was still my mother.

In March 2015, I received a call from a hospital in Mississippi that would change everything. My mom had suffered a stroke, and before that, her kidneys had failed, requiring her to start dialysis. The doctor's voice on the other end of the line was grave, explaining that her condition was dire and that she might not make it. As I listened, I felt the weight of all the years, all the pain, all the history between us bearing down on me.

I had spent two years in a shelter by then, a time that had allowed me to heal mentally and save some money, but I wasn't prepared for what came next. The decision to bring my mom back to Minnesota was both instinctual and terrifying. Despite everything, I knew I couldn't let her go through this alone in a place far from family. I spent the next week on the phone, calling everyone I could to make arrangements. I used up all my savings to fly her back and find us a place to live. I moved us into a five-bedroom, two-bathroom duplex, doing everything I could to create a stable environment where I could care for her.

Looking back, I can now see that God never left me, He was right there with me, preparing me for this moment. Every struggle, heartbreak, and lesson shaped me into the person I needed to become—not just for myself but for my children and, ultimately, for my mother. The challenges I faced weren't just about surviving; they were about equipping me with the tools to navigate a life filled with complexity and contradiction.

It wasn't just the thought of the possible difficulties of caring for my mother that tested me—it was the emotional weight of reconciling my past with her. Caring for a woman who had caused me so much pain, yet whom I still loved, required a depth of compassion I wasn't sure I had. But the mental healing I experienced during my time in the shelter gave me a new capacity for grace. It softened my heart in ways I didn't expect. Without that season of healing, I'm not sure I would've been able to see my mother as anything more than the woman who had failed me.

Her struggles didn't excuse the past, but they helped me understand her in a way I never could before. I realized that loving someone doesn't mean denying their faults. It means embracing the entirety of who they are—the good, the bad, and everything in between.

I finally understood the meaning of the popular modern Christian allegory *Footprints in the Sand*. For so long, I'd felt abandoned, weighed down by life's hardships, wondering why I had to endure so much. But reflecting on my journey, I could see that I was never truly alone. When life felt unbearable, when I questioned, *"Why me?"*—a better question emerged: *"Why not me?"*

God had been with me through every walk of life, even when I couldn't see it. The obstacles, grief, and uncertainty weren't meant to break me; they were shaping me for something greater. At the time, the pain felt senseless, but now I understand that some of life's toughest battles are preparation for a purpose far beyond what we can imagine.

Everything I had been through made me who I am today. Every tear, every loss, every dark night of the soul played a part in molding me into someone strong enough to carry not just my burdens but those of the people I love. I didn't just survive—I grew, I learned, and I became. And through it all, even in the silence, even when I felt forgotten, God was there, carrying me when I couldn't walk on my own.

Taking care of my mom became my full-time job. It was overwhelming, exhausting, and yet, in some ways, it was healing. For the first time, we spent time together—real time. We had long conversations about the past, her regrets, her struggles. We laughed and cried, sharing moments that had been absent for so long. One of our favorite things to do was watch movies and eat together. In those small moments, I felt a closeness that I had always longed for, even if it was fleeting.

But the reality of her declining health quickly overshadowed these moments. My mom had a long list of health issues that only seemed to grow with each passing year. When she first moved in with us, I had hoped that being surrounded by family would lift her spirits, but her body was betraying her. The tasks she once did effortlessly became monumental challenges. It was hard for her to accept, and even harder for me to watch. She clung to the belief that she could still manage, but it became clear that she couldn't.

One day, while I was at work, my mom decided to fry some chicken. It was something she had done a million times before, but this time, something went wrong. The stove caught fire, and smoke filled the kitchen. My kids were home at the time, and I can only imagine the fear they must have felt. When I got the call, my heart sank. I rushed home, terrified of what I might find, and it was then I knew I had to make a decision. As much as it hurt, I couldn't keep her safe at home anymore. The fear of what could happen next was too much to bear.

I moved her into an assisted living facility, hoping it would provide the balance she needed—independence with support. But not long after she moved in, she caught the stove on fire again. Her physical decline continued, and her mental state followed. She had several falls, and soon, the staff suggested moving her to a nursing home. It felt like defeat, but I knew it was necessary. My mom, however, didn't see it that way. She was devastated and angry, mostly at me. No matter what I did, she was never happy. The woman who had always prided herself on her independence was now reliant on others for everything, and it was crushing her.

Her decline wasn't just physical. She began missing her dialysis appointments, and when the toxins started building up in her system, it was as though I was watching her slip away piece by piece. The confusion, the forgetfulness—it was like dementia, but worse because I knew it was preventable. Without dialysis, her body was failing her. Painful blisters formed on her skin, bursting and leaving open sores that refused to heal due to her diabetes. She was always in pain, and there was little I could do to alleviate it.

The nursing home did their best, but they couldn't give her the intensive care she needed when she refused dialysis. Each time she missed a session, the toxins would accumulate, leading to another trip to the hospital. Each hospital visit felt like another battle, pulling her back from the brink of death only for her to refuse the care that would keep her alive. I was losing her, not just to her illness, but to a part of her that seemed to no longer want to fight.

And that's why we're here again, in the hospital. The nursing home had reached their limits, and now it was up to me to watch her fade, to fight for her care, and to navigate the heartache of losing her bit by bit. It was the hardest thing I had ever done, but I knew it was what I was meant to do. God had prepared me for this, even when I didn't realize it.

Chapter Six: Between Life and Loss

Now, two days later, I have been tossing and turning all night with uncontrollable gas pains, probably because I worked a late shift. I don't have much of an appetite and I've been eating antacids like Skittles, but it hasn't helped much. My phone rings, and it is my sister-in-law checking on me to make sure I made it home safe from my road trip yesterday.

"Hey, how are you feeling?" she asks, her voice filled with concern.

"I don't know, I've got these bad gas pains," I reply, wincing. "I've been eating antacids like they're candy, but they're not working."

"Did you eat something weird on the road trip?" she asks.

"I don't think so. I haven't had much of an appetite. I think I need something stronger than antacids," I say, trying to keep my voice steady.

"I doubt it's anything serious, but better safe than sorry. How about I take you to the ER? Just to be sure," she suggests.

"Yeah, maybe that's a good idea," I admit reluctantly. "I can't take this pain much longer."

"Alright, I'll be over in a few minutes. Hang in there," she reassures me before hanging up.

I sigh, feeling a mix of relief and anxiety. I hope it is just a simple case of indigestion, but a part of me couldn't shake the feeling that something is seriously wrong.

By the time we made it into the ER, my gas pains had gotten stronger for some reason. Because I am pregnant, I have to go to the labor and delivery floor. I start to feel nauseous and weak. They follow the normal protocol and connect me to a fetal monitor.

A nurse comes in and asks me to describe what I am feeling as she looks at the monitor with concern.

"Can you tell me what you're experiencing?" she asks.

"I've got these gas pains that are making me feel nauseous," I explain, trying to steady my voice. "They're putting pressure on my back too."

The nurse's expression changes as she examines the monitor. "Honey," she says gently, "you're in labor."

"What? But that is not possible! I'm only 26 weeks pregnant."

The nurse nods sympathetically, "I understand this is a shock. Let's get you stabilized and make sure everything is okay with the baby."

As a wave of fear and disbelief washes over me, I struggle to process what is happening.

How could this be happening now?

I try to calm my racing thoughts, but worry clings to me like wet clothes, as they prepare to address the unexpected situation. This is my fourth child, and every other pregnancy has been smooth, leading to healthy, full-term babies. The suddenness of this complication feels like a nightmare I can't wake up from.

After checking on the baby, the doctor reassures me that everything seems fine for now. They administer IV medication to halt the contractions, and then tell me the news that I'd need to stay in the hospital for a few days. My immediate reaction is panic. I am not prepared for this.

My kids, my mom—what was I going to do?

I quickly arrange for my kids' grandparents to step in, knowing I can count on them to keep things stable at home. My relationship with my fourth child's father is far from ideal; he isn't much help, and I feel the weight of responsibility entirely on my shoulders. Once I made sure my kids were taken care of, I turned my attention to my mom.

Calling her at the hospital, I try to explain what is happening, though I am not sure how much she truly understood. Her health had deteriorated significantly, and I knew her mental clarity came and went. When I told her about the premature labor, her response was surprisingly indifferent, almost disconnected from the gravity of the situation. "Okay," she says casually, "so, when you are done, are you going to bring me some chicken?"

Her words sting, not because of what she said, but because they remind me of how far gone she is. Here I am, facing one of the most terrifying moments of my life, and my mother—

my once-strong, resilient mother—could only think about something as trivial as food. I try to push the hurt aside, focusing on the situation at hand.

For three long days, the hospital staff work tirelessly to stop my labor. The IV medications keep the contractions at bay, but the moment they discontinued them, the contractions returned with a vengeance. By the fourth day, I am exhausted—physically, emotionally, and mentally. I am still contracting, but I haven't dilated, and the nurses informed me that they are going to discharge me.

Frustration and anxiety simmer just beneath the surface. I am in pain, stuck in the hospital, and away from my kids when they need me. To make matters worse, my mom has been calling me every hour, confused and upset, wondering why I wasn't coming to see her. Since she's moved out of my house, I never go more than two days without visiting her, except for a brief road trip to Chicago right before this crisis. Now, the distance is taking its toll on her. She is growing more hostile and confused with each call, likely feeling abandoned despite my reassurances that I'd visit her as soon as I could. Her calls, once a source of comfort, have become a reminder of how deeply intertwined our lives still are, even in the midst of this chaos.

When the nurses come in with the discharge paperwork, I can barely stand. The pain in my body is a constant, throbbing reminder that something isn't right. I tell them how much pain I am in, but their response is disheartening. They say there is nothing they can do because my labor is not progressing, and by protocol, they can't keep me there.

A small part of me feels a glimmer of relief at the thought of finally leaving the hospital. I can go see my mom, ease her worries, and maybe, just maybe, find some comfort in her presence. But underneath that relief is a growing fear. This cannot be normal. The pain is overwhelming, and the thought of leaving the hospital in such a state is unsettling. Yet, I have no choice. I am being sent home.

As I begin to put my clothes on, a wave of pressure suddenly hits me, radiating through my pelvic area with an intensity that makes me wince. I struggle to dress myself, every movement sending fresh jolts of pain through my body. I have an urgent need to use the restroom, so I wobble to the bathroom, hunched over, each step a battle against the pain. The pressure is building, and as I make my way back to the bed, a disturbing urge to push overcomes me. Panic sets in. I grab the side of the bed, my knuckles turning white as I try to steady myself, and yell for help. My voice trembles with fear as I feel a warm liquid start to run down my leg. I am too terrified to look down.

A nurse rushes in, her face a mixture of concern and urgency. She quickly helps me into the bed, and the moment I lay down, the pain escalates to a level I have never experienced before. It is excruciating, beyond anything I can imagine. In this moment, I would do anything to make it stop, even if it meant giving up.

I scream, my voice cracking with desperation, begging them to give me something, anything, to ease the pain. The room quickly fills with nurses, about eight of them, each moving with practiced speed and precision. Some are cutting my clothes off, others are trying to get an IV back into my arm. The room is a blur of activity, voices shouting codes, numbers, and medical terms that I can't comprehend. The commotion is overwhelming, the sheer intensity of it all crashing down on me like a wave.

And then, suddenly, everything goes black.

When I wake up, the chaos has been replaced by an eerie calm. I am in surgery, surrounded by the soft glow of overhead lights. The pain is gone, replaced by a strange sense of peace. I can see the doctors working above me, their faces focused and serene. I tried to move, but my body feels heavy, as if I am floating just beneath the surface of consciousness. But I don't want to move. I don't want to disrupt the tranquility that has settled over me. The contrast between the serenity of the moment and the nightmare I had just lived through is jarring, yet oddly comforting.

All I want to do is close my eyes, let the peace envelop me, and rest.

I wake up in recovery, trying to piece together what has just happened. The nurse comes in and immediately apologizes. She looks as if she has been crying.

Nurse: "I'm so sorry. You suffered a placenta abruption."

Me: "I have no idea what that is, but I know it was painful."

The surgeon comes in next.

Surgeon: "The surgery went well. You did lose a lot of blood, but you didn't need a transfusion."

As they start to unplug things to take me to my room, the nurse asks me a question that takes me by surprise.

Nurse: "Would you like to see your baby?"

Me: "No, thank you. I'm not ready to see my baby's little body."

Nurse: "Okay. When you are ready, the NICU is..."

I cut her off, confused.

Me: "Wait, the NICU?"

Nurse: "Yes."

Me: "That's where the babies are that are alive?"

Nurse: "Yes, your beautiful baby girl is in the NICU."

I start crying tears of joy.

Me: "Of course, I want to see her!"

When we arrive at the NICU, I am met with a sight that takes my breath away. There, nestled in an incubator, is the smallest human being I have ever laid eyes on—my daughter. She weighs just 2 pounds and 3 ounces, a fragile little bundle of life. Her tiny chest rises and falls with each delicate breath, and I can see the translucent skin stretching over her minuscule limbs. As I sit there, staring at her through the glass, every bit of pain and fear I have endured seems to melt away. This is my baby, my miracle, and in that moment, I feel the profound weight of what has just happened. March 5th, 2018, will forever be etched in my memory as the day I witnessed, firsthand, the power of God and the incredible advancements of modern medicine.

But the joy of her birth has been tempered by the harsh reality of our situation. A few days later, I was discharged from the hospital—a day that should have been filled with relief and happiness. Instead, it is bittersweet. I have to leave my tiny daughter behind in the NICU, her incubator, the only home she knows. The thought of going home without her is agonizing. My heart aches as I walk out of the hospital, knowing she will be there, fighting to grow stronger without me by her side.

Back home, there is no time to rest. My other children need me, and so does my mom. I am being pulled in every direction, with little to no help to share the burden. My life feels like it is spinning out of control, each day blending into the next with an exhausting rhythm. I am torn between the hospital and home, and it seems like there is no time to catch my breath. But there is no option to slow down; I have to keep moving forward.

My days have become a whirlwind of responsibilities. I start each morning by spending time with my kids, making sure they are settled for the day. Then I rush to see my mom, checking in on her at the nursing home, before heading back to the hospital to be with my preemie. At the NICU, I pump milk, sit by her side, and pray for her to grow stronger. After that, it is back home to get my other children ready for the night, making sure they feel my presence and love despite everything going on. And when they are finally asleep, I return to the hospital, staying by my daughter's side through the long, quiet hours of the night.

Each day, the cycle repeats. It is a relentless grind that leaves me physically and emotionally drained. Time seems to blur together, the days passing in a haze of exhaustion and worry. Yet, as overwhelming as it all is, I can't afford to stop. I have to be there for everyone, holding my family together while managing the chaos of my own emotions.

The weeks slip by faster than I can comprehend, and before I know it, we are nearing the end of April. I can barely remember how we've gotten here.

The weight of being my mother's power of attorney has become almost unbearable because she told me she is tired of dialysis and doesn't want to do it anymore. It feels like the world is crashing down around me as I realize that I am the one who has to make the decision. I immediately reach out to my siblings, hoping for some guidance, some shared burden, but deep down, I already know what I am going to do.

"Absolutely not!" I thought. The very idea of her stopping dialysis sends a cold shiver down my spine. If she stops, her body wouldn't be able to filter the toxins, and her organs would begin to shut down, one by one. That is unthinkable. I am desperate for more time with her.

How could I let her go without hearing her say she was proud of me?

There are so many things left unsaid, so many questions I still have. I don't care if she is often difficult to deal with or if she is mean at times. The idea of losing her, of not having her in my life at all, is more than I can bear.

What would I do without her?

I rush to the hospital, filled with a mix of determination and fear. I sit by her bed and plead with her to keep fighting. "Mom, please keep doing dialysis. Don't you want to live?" I ask, my voice trembling with emotion.

"Yes, I want to live. I am strong," she replies, trying to muster the strength that I know is slipping away from her.

But later that day, when I get back home, the doctor calls to tell me she is refusing again. My heart sinks, and I refuse to believe it. I convince myself that the staff is just tired of dealing with her and that they are lying to me. My mom wouldn't say that. She just told me she wants to live! I demand they put the phone in her room, and when I hear her voice on the other end, my denial crumbles. She is begging them to let her stop dialysis.

I am crushed. This woman who has always been a pillar of strength in my life is now tired of the fight. She has been holding on for me, trying to stay strong because she knows how much I need her. But she didn't have the strength to tell me she is ready to let go.

Her condition has deteriorated so much. She can no longer walk or stand, and her big toe on her left foot has been amputated. Her legs are constantly wrapped because of open blisters that never seem to heal. She is always itchy, in pain, and the slightest touch feels like knives piercing her skin. Dialysis is a brutal routine, 4-5 days a week, and she has lost so much weight that I can lift her with ease. The realization hits me like a ton of bricks—how selfish I have been! This is torture for her, and yet I am clinging to her for my own reasons.

The thought makes me sick to my stomach. I want her to stay because I can't imagine life without her, not because it is what is best for her. And that realization, more than anything, is the hardest thing to accept.

I take a deep breath, trying to steady myself as I walk into the hospital room. My heart is heavy with the weight of what I am about to ask. I look at her, my mother—the woman who has always seemed invincible to me—and I feel my throat tighten. "Mom," I begin, my voice barely above a whisper, "are you trying to be strong for me?" Her eyes meet mine, and I see tears slowly making their way down her worn face. In that moment, it feels like time stands still, and the distance between us is filled with the unspoken pain of what we both know is coming.

I cannot avoid the truth any longer. "Do you know what will happen if you stop dialysis?" I ask, needing to hear her say it out loud, to confront the reality of her decision. She nods, a small, almost imperceptible movement, and whispers, "Yes."

"What will happen, Mom?" I press, though every part of me dreads hearing the answer.

"I will die," she says, her voice steady but laced with the sadness of acceptance.

The world around me seems to fall away in this moment. The sounds of the hospital, the hum of machines, the murmur of voices in the hallway—they all fade into the background as I grapple with the enormity of her words. I feel an overwhelming mixture of pride and sorrow as I look at her, this incredibly strong woman who has faced more than her fair share of battles, now choosing to let go.

I try to keep my voice steady as I tell her how much I admire her strength, how she has overcome so many obstacles in life. "Mom, be honest with me," I pleaded. "Do you really want to stop dialysis?"

She doesn't hesitate this time. Her eyes are full of tears as she nods and whispers, "Yes."

It feels like the earth shifted beneath my feet. My heart shatters into pieces, yet there is a strange calm that settles over me as well. I am proud of her for being vulnerable, for admitting that she is ready to stop fighting, but the pain of losing her is almost unbearable. As I stand there, frozen by the reality of what is to come, she reaches out her hand towards me. It is a gesture so simple, yet so profound.

My mother has never been one for physical affection, and I hesitate, unsure of what she wants. I know how much she hurts, and that even the slightest touch could bring her agony. But at this moment, I realize that she isn't asking for relief from her pain—she is asking for comfort, for connection. I slowly lean in, uncertain, and she wraps her frail arms around me, pulling me closer. I lay my head on her chest, feeling her heartbeat beneath my ear, and she whispers softly, "It will be okay, baby."

That is all it takes. The tears I have been holding back for so long come pouring out, a torrent of grief and love and fear. My mind goes blank; there are no more words, no more thoughts. Just the feeling of my mother's arms around me, holding me as I cry for the loss that hasn't yet come but feels all too real.

Chapter Seven: Last Goodbye

The next day, I gather my strength and do what needs to be done. I call my siblings and tell them about my decision to start her on hospice care. It is the hardest thing I've ever had to do, but I know it is the right thing. The adrenaline that has kept me going for months is still there, pushing me forward, because even though my heart is breaking, life didn't stop. My baby is going to be discharged from the NICU soon, and now I have to plan for my mother's last days.

When my siblings arrive, we spend as much time as we can with her. We fill the room with her favorite songs, and even in her weakened state, she tries to sing along, her voice cracking with effort. She even tries to dance a little, a small smile on her face as she swayed gently in her chair. These moments are bittersweet—precious memories that I know will carry me through the darkest days ahead.

As soon as my daughter is finally discharged, I bring her to meet my mom. She is still so tiny, just 3 months old and barely 5 pounds. My mom smiles as she looks at her, a soft laugh escaping her lips as she says, "She looks like a little frog with those long arms and legs." For a moment, it feels like things might be okay. My mom even starts to feel better, or at least she says she does. The itching isn't as bad, and she hasn't taken as many pain medications. Hope begins to creep in. Maybe, just maybe, she is getting better. Maybe God is performing a miracle. After all, who better to receive a miracle than my mom?

But it wasn't to be. My hope is nothing more than wishful thinking, a desperate attempt to hold on to her for just a little while longer. On June 3, 2018, my mother passed away. The loss is profound, and the grief comes in waves, but I am grateful for the time we had, for the moments of connection and love in her final days. She is my mom, my strength, and even in her last breath, she taught me about courage, love, and the power of letting go.

As we prepare for the funeral, I find myself moving through the motions as if on autopilot. I am numb—completely disconnected from the reality of what is happening. It is as if my mind has constructed a barrier between me and the overwhelming emotions that threaten to consume me. I have just brought my preemie baby home, a moment that should have been filled with joy, but instead, I am surrounded by the heavy fog of grief. My siblings have flown in from out of town, and while it is comforting to have them close, I feel like a ghost in my own life. I long to retreat to my bed, to hide from the world and the unbearable truth that my mother is really gone.

My children are full of questions, their innocent curiosity piercing through the haze I am trying to maintain. I thought I had done the right thing by shielding them from my mom's decline, wanting them to remember her as the lively, fun granny they adored, not as the fragile, sick woman she has become. But now, as I face their questions, I am not so sure. My second child took the loss especially hard. She and my mom had been inseparable—best friends in a way that transcended generations. She didn't understand why her granny was gone and, in her young mind, she blames me for putting her in a nursing home. She even blames the doctors, convinced they could have fixed her if only they had tried harder. It breaks my heart to see her struggling with grief that she couldn't fully comprehend.

The combination of my mother's death and the demands of caring for a preemie has left me utterly exhausted. I haven't had a good night's sleep in months, my body and mind running on nothing but adrenaline and the sheer will to keep going. But now, the day I have been dreading has arrived—the day we lay my mother to rest. Despite my emotional numbness, I have to admit that everything looks beautiful. My brothers and my oldest brother's wife, Jane, have taken care of all the arrangements, and they have done an incredible job.

The morning of the funeral is a blur. We gather at the funeral home for the viewing, and the room slowly fills with familiar faces—old childhood friends, members of my mom's church, members from my own church, and close friends who have come to support us. I stand in the entranceway of the funeral home, trying to keep myself together, when Jane comes over to me. She asks if I have taken a moment to view my mom yet. I nod, telling her that I have briefly looked at her and how beautiful she looks. Jane gently reminds me that once the casket closes, we would have the service and then head to the burial site, so this is my last chance to say goodbye.

It is as if a switch has flipped in my mind. Suddenly, everything becomes painfully real. In just a few minutes, I will be seeing my mother's face for the very last time. The weight of that realization hits me like a ton of bricks. My chest tightens, and my legs feel weak as I force myself to walk over to the casket. As I stand there, looking down at her, I am struck by how peaceful she appears. The lines of pain and suffering that have etched her face for so long are gone, replaced by a serene expression that I haven't seen in years. She looks beautiful, just as she always has, but now she is free from the struggles that have defined her final years. I lean in closer, wanting to memorize every detail of her face, to hold onto this last image of her.

I whisper a final goodbye, my voice trembling as the tears I have been holding back begin to flow. I know she isn't in pain anymore, that she is at peace, but that didn't make letting go any easier. As I stand there, the reality of her absence settles over me like a heavy blanket, and I realize that this was the end of an era in my life. She is gone, and with her went a part of me that I would never get back. But even in this moment of profound loss, there is a strange comfort in knowing that she is finally at rest, she is no longer suffering. The pastor announces that we would be starting the service and asks everyone to take a seat.

My body feels paralyzed, like my feet are glued to the floor. I stare at my mother's casket, knowing that as soon as I walk away, this chapter of my life will close forever. The finality of it all weighs on me like an anchor. I am not ready to let go—not yet, not ever. I thought I was prepared for this moment, but as I stand there, I realize just how wrong I am. The pastor's voice cuts through my thoughts, asking everyone to take their seats once more, but I can't comply. I look up at him, shaking my head slightly, as if I could somehow stop time from moving forward.
Tears begin to spill down my face, and I lower my head, silently pleading, *Please, Lord, let me wake up from this nightmare.* The room falls into an eerie silence, the kind that makes every second feel like an eternity. Then, I feel hands gently grasping my arms, one on each side. I don't need to look to know who it is—my sister, Trish, always the one to comfort me in my

darkest moments. She leans in close, whispering softly in my ear, "Come on, baby girl." Her words, so tender, are the catalyst that unleashes the flood of emotions I have been holding back. My silent tears turn into a gut-wrenching outcry, a primal scream that echoes through the room. "NO!!! Please, no! Just wait… Wait!"

The anger inside me swells like a storm. I am not just sad or hurt—I am furious.

How could she do this to me? How could she leave me again?

It feels like all those other times she had left, but this time, I know there is no coming back. If I could just stand there a little longer, maybe, just maybe, I could steal a few more moments with her. But Trish, ever gentle and understanding, begins to guide me away from the casket. As I turn around, I catch sight of my children. Their faces are pale, stricken with shock, their eyes wide with tears. They look at me as if I have become a stranger, someone they didn't recognize. I realize then that they have never seen me cry before—not like this.

I have always been the strong one, the pillar they could lean on. Tears have always felt like a luxury I couldn't afford, a sign of weakness that I have worked so hard to keep hidden. But in this moment, every wall I have built around my emotions crumbled. Unable to bear it any longer, I bolt from the room, my heart pounding in my chest like a drum. I run to the bathroom, gasping for breath as a full-blown panic attack takes hold of me. The walls seem to close in, and the weight of everything that has happened presses down on me with unbearable force. It feels like my world is spinning out of control, and I can't find my footing.

I miss the first half of the funeral, locked in the bathroom, struggling to pull myself back together. When I finally re-enter the room, I see my second daughter standing at the front, reading a scripture. The sight of her there, so poised and strong, fills me with a bittersweet pride. Granny would be so proud of her, I think, my heart swells with love and sorrow in equal measure. Lamar's speech follows, and it is nothing short of phenomenal. He captures the essence of who my mother is, painting a vivid picture of her life and the impact she has had on everyone she meets. His words give substance to her memory, filling the room with a sense of her presence that is both comforting and heartbreaking.

After the service, we share hugs and whispered words of comfort, each of us trying to make sense of the loss we are feeling. Then, it is time to head to the burial site. The drive there feels surreal, the reality of what is happening sinking in with every passing minute. The final goodbye is approaching, and though I have made it through the service, I know that laying her to rest will be the hardest part yet. At the burial site, as the cemetery employees explain how my mother's gravesite will be maintained and provide details about visiting hours, I listen but feel distant, as if I am watching everything unfold from behind a glass wall.

My mind is elsewhere. Family members speak a few heartfelt words, and the weight of the moment seems to settle over us all, heavy and suffocating. Then, off in the distance, a small, vibrant blue butterfly catches my eye. At first, I paid it no mind. It is summer, after all, and butterflies are a common sight. There is nothing unusual about a butterfly flitting about on a warm day like this. But as I watch, the butterfly begins to make its way toward us, its delicate wings catching the sunlight as it flies.

I still don't think much of it— perhaps it is simply looking for a place to rest. To my surprise, the butterfly flies straight to my mother's casket and lands gently on top. It rests there for a moment, its bright blue wings contrasting against the somberness of the scene. I can't help but notice how peaceful it looks, almost as if it belongs there. But even then, I don't dwell on it; butterflies land on flowers, on leaves, on anything that catches their fancy. Why not a casket?

But then, the butterfly begins to move, fluttering off the casket and making its way around the circle of family members who have gathered to say their final goodbyes. It dances through the air, moving from person to person, as if it was deliberately visiting each one of us. The grandchildren and cousins are enchanted, holding out their hands as the butterfly lands on them and then takes flight again, eliciting smiles and laughter amid the tears. It is a beautiful moment, a brief but welcome distraction from the grief that hangs in the air. For everyone else, the butterfly is a sign of beauty and grace, something to marvel at. But for me, it is a source of unease. I have always been terrified of anything that flies, slithers, crawls, or walks—especially insects.

So, when the butterfly flies in my direction, I instinctively step back, wanting to give it plenty of space to move along. I assume it would continue its journey around the circle and leave me alone, but it doesn't. The butterfly turns around and flies straight back toward me. I move in the opposite direction, hoping to avoid it, but again it follows. This happens once more, and with nowhere else to go, I can feel my anxiety rising. The last thing I want is for this creature to land on me. I decide to slowly jog out of the way, thinking that would surely send the butterfly in another direction. But it is as if the butterfly had other plans. It continues to chase me, as if it has something to prove or perhaps a message to deliver. I am terrified, my heart racing, but something inside me tells me to stop running. So, I stand still, bracing myself for what feels like the inevitable.

The butterfly hovers for a moment, then gently lands on my back. It is a strange feeling, a mix of fear and calmness washing over me simultaneously. It stays there for a brief moment, then lifts off and flies away. As soon as it leaves, I couldn't shake the feeling that there is something significant about this butterfly. It isn't just an ordinary insect—it feels like a sign, something more profound than a simple coincidence. I can't stop thinking about it, so later that day, I looked it up. To my astonishment, I discovered that the type of butterfly I saw wasn't native to Minnesota. The more I think about it, the more it seems impossible—yet it has happened, and I wasn't the only one who had seen it.

The entire family had witnessed this strange and beautiful moment. In that instant, I was convinced that the butterfly was more than just a creature passing by. I believe it was my mother, coming back in a form I would never have expected, to let us know that she was okay and that we would be okay too. The symbolism of the butterfly is powerful—it represents transformation, change, and the journey from one stage of life to another. It embodies growth, evolution, and the beauty that can emerge from challenges and transitions. In many cultures, butterflies are seen as a sign of hope and new beginnings, a reminder that life goes on and that there is beauty even in the midst of sorrow.

It would be just like my mom to come back as something I find terrifying, like a butterfly, to reassure me that everything would be alright. It was her way of reminding me that even in her absence, she was still looking out for me, still finding ways to connect with me. That butterfly, in all its delicate persistence, was my mother's final message to me: Be strong, move forward, and remember that I am always with you. As I begin this next chapter, I find myself reflecting on the lessons learned from my mother's life— the mistakes she made and the strengths she possessed.

Everything I went through, all the trials and tribulations, has molded me into the person I am today. And while I used to pride myself on not being like her, I now realize that fragments of who she was has become integral pieces of who I am. My mother's mistakes, the ones that caused so much pain and confusion, also taught me resilience and determination. Her struggles pushed me to be better, to ensure that my children have a life filled with opportunities I never had. I've made it my mission to pour every ounce of energy into them, guiding them toward a brighter future.

Chapter Eight: Breaking the Cycle

Having children at a young age was a journey marked by so many unknowns—an endless cycle of lessons learned on the fly, hopes stitched together with anxieties. My oldest, Alicia, and I grew up together in many ways. I was just 20, juggling a toddler and a newborn with only a vague sense of how to balance their needs. I assumed my younger one required my undivided attention, so as long as Alicia was fed, bathed, clothed, and had what she needed for school, I thought she would be okay. I didn't fully grasp then how much weight my assumptions would place on her small shoulders.

Alicia, though still so young, became more than a big sister. By the time she was seven, she had slipped into roles no child should have to. She helped with her siblings, and there were days when her maturity was startling, an old soul in the body of a child. I leaned on her too heavily—not because I wanted to, but because I was just trying to keep our heads above water, overwhelmed by motherhood, work, and a constant undercurrent of fear that seemed to follow us.

My anxiety seeped into every aspect of our lives, shaping our routines, decisions, and interactions. I couldn't let my children out of my sight unless they were with their fathers, and even then, I struggled with gnawing fears of the unknown. Having seen and felt too much of what could go wrong, I was hyper-aware of every potential danger the world held. The safest place for my kids was always close to me. My love was fierce, but my protectiveness cast a shadow, creating a home that, while filled with love, often felt confined. My children were never far, almost orbiting around my anxieties, growing up in a world shaped as much by my care as by my caution.

In my pursuit of being a "great mom," I pushed myself to work multiple jobs and attend school, convinced that financial stability was the key to a better life for my children. But my deep-rooted fears and inability to fully trust anyone with their care led me to only sending them to daycare until I believed they were old enough to handle being alone safely. That decision kept them safe under my wing but also meant they watched me push through a storm of stress, trauma, and relentless hardships.

I spent every day working toward an idea I thought would erase the pain I'd known growing up. My dream was clear: a big house, a perfect family, maybe even that white picket fence. But it wasn't as simple as chasing a dream; it was an effort to rewrite my past, thinking that creating the life I'd never had would mean success.

Reflecting now, especially after my mother passed, I see that life wasn't simply about paying bills or filling our home with things. In the shelter, something unexpected happened. We had nothing but each other, yet those were some of the happiest days we spent together. I didn't have to leave for work or run between jobs. I didn't have much to give, but we had time—a gift I'd hardly realized we needed until it was almost too late. For so many years, I had focused on "providing" for my kids. I believed they needed things: toys, clothes, and a perfect future. But looking back, the most valuable thing I could have given them was simply to be present.

Since I wasn't working, I was able to do the small things that I had never had time for—waking them up in the morning, getting them ready for school, picking them up from the bus stop, having dinner together, even attending school field trips. I hadn't realized how much I had been missing out on until I was forced to slow down. That time showed me how disconnected I had been, and I began to truly see my kids for the first time.

One day, Alicia, who had always carried the weight of being mature beyond her years, got upset with me. I can't remember the specifics of what triggered it, but I will never forget what she said. She yelled, "I don't care about any of the stuff you buy me! All I wanted was your time! But it's too late now, I'm okay with the way things have been."

At first, I was shocked—*Who the hell was she talking to?* But then I looked at her and saw the pain in her eyes. She wasn't just being angry; she was hurt. She had carried the weight of my absence.

Even though I was there, I wasn't there you know what I mean?

The clothes, toys, and gadgets I had worked so hard to provide didn't matter to her. What she had really wanted all along was my time—my undivided attention, my presence.

It wasn't until that moment that I truly understood how much my absence had affected her. I could see the resentment and frustration in her actions, she had likely been holding onto for years. Her distant and sometimes annoyed attitude suddenly made sense. Instead of reacting defensively, I chose to acknowledge her pain. I apologized and let her know that I would do everything in my power to change, to be more present, to give her the time and love she needed.

I had spent so long trying not to be like my mother, thinking that avoiding her mistakes meant I was doing right by my kids. My focus was on making sure they didn't go without, and to me, that meant financial security. But in my attempt to avoid one type of failure, I had missed the importance of emotional presence. I realized that, like my mother, I had been so consumed with survival that I forgot the importance of nurturing.

I was introduced to a home visiting nurse named Jeanne Kumlin during my first pregnancy. Her agency was among the other resources I was receiving to help me have a successful pregnancy. My time with her is when I began to truly understand what it meant to be a mother. Jeanne wasn't just checking in on my health or my babies' health; she was teaching me, supporting me, and guiding me. She spoke life into me, telling me I was doing great even when I felt the opposite. There was this unforgettable moment I experienced with her. At that time I had my first apartment, It was small and wasn't in the greatest neighborhood but it was mine. I was sitting in my tiny, cozy living room with toys scattered on the floor. The faint smell of baby lotion lingered in the air. The afternoon sun filtered through sheer curtains. I heard a knock at the door.

It was Jeanne there for our regular meeting that I totally forgot about. She arrived at my door with her usual warm smile, her short pixie-cut hair perfectly styled and her eyes filled with warmth. She carried her worn leather bag, always ready to help in whatever way she could. Just seeing her on my doorstep made my chest loosen, even if only for a moment.

Inside, chaos was in full swing. Two-year-old Alicia was in the middle of one of her epic tantrums, kicking and screaming on the floor. Ta'Nyla, just a newborn, was softly wailing in her bassinet, her tiny fists flailing in frustration. Ta'nyla as an infant had the quietest cry, I sometimes wouldn't know she was crying until I walked past her. So I always had to continuously check on her. I was running on fumes, juggling cries from both of them while feeling utterly defeated.

Jeanne stepped in without hesitation, her voice soft and steady. "Hey there, Mama. Looks like it's been a tough morning."

I nodded, already on the verge of tears. "She's been like this all day," I confessed, glancing at Alicia, who was now laying on her back and flopping around like a fish out of water.. "I can't get her to stop. And the baby—she's not sleeping much. I'm just... I don't know what I'm doing."

Jeanne gently touched my arm. "You're doing more than you realize," she said firmly. "Let's take it one step at a time."

She crouched down to Alicia's level, her soothing presence cutting through the storm. "Alicia, sweetheart," she said softly, "are you feeling upset right now?"

Alicia paused mid-sob, curiosity momentarily overtaking her anger. She sniffled but didn't respond.

"That's okay," Jeanne continued gently. "It's hard being two sometimes, isn't it?"

I watched, stunned by how Alicia seemed to calm under Jeanne's calm gaze. It was like watching magic happen right before me.

Turning back to me, Jeanne smiled. "Toddlers have big feelings that they don't know how to handle yet. When she's calm, try getting on her level like this and naming what she might be feeling."

I wiped my face, overwhelmed but hopeful. "And the baby? She's up all night...I'm so tired."

Jeanne nodded sympathetically. "Let's try adjusting her nighttime routine—maybe a warm bath before bed, some gentle rocking...we'll figure it out together."

Her words felt like a lifeline thrown just when I thought I was drowning. She wasn't judging me or pointing out what I was doing wrong. She was showing me how to move forward with patience and love, something I hadn't felt in a long time.

Jeanne saw me—not just as a struggling young mom—but as someone capable, someone worth investing in. And in that moment, I felt just a little bit stronger.

As I grew, I realized that being a good mother wasn't just about not repeating my mother's mistakes. It was about learning from them, building on them, and creating something better for my own children. I had inherited some of her drive, but I had also gained the tools to nurture my children in ways that she hadn't been able to.

This realization has given me the ability to approach motherhood with a sense of purpose and gratitude. Despite the hardships, I'm thankful for what I've learned, and I strive to give my children not just financial security but the emotional presence and love they deserve.

My oldest, at just 18, is a brilliant and goal-driven young woman with a deep passion for animals. From an early age, it was clear she had a special connection with them, and that bond has only grown stronger over the years. She's set to graduate this coming May 2024 with a bachelor's degree in Animal Science—a remarkable achievement made even more impressive by the fact that she accomplished this while still in high school. By the time she graduated high school, she had already completed two years of college, a testament to her relentless drive and focus.

With a 3.9 GPA, she's on track to be one of the youngest Veterinarian doctors in Minnesota if she's accepted into Veterinary school, which I have no doubt she will be. Her dedication and unwavering love for animals inspire me every day. Watching her pursue her dreams with such determination fills me with pride and awe.

Our relationship has blossomed into something truly special, and I continue to work on nurturing that bond daily. She's self-sufficient, financially stable, and wise beyond her years. Seeing her handle life with such maturity and grace makes me incredibly proud of the young woman she has become. I couldn't be more proud of her and all the hard work she has put in to reach this point. Her future is bright, and I know she's destined for greatness.

Then there's my 16-year-old, my mini-me. She embodies everything I could hope for in a daughter—responsible, helpful, and incredibly driven. Recently, she achieved a major milestone by getting her driver's license and her first car, a moment that symbolized her growing independence. But she didn't stop there. She balances a full-time job with maintaining her spot on the A/B honor roll, showing a level of discipline and focus that's rare at her age.

Despite her busy schedule, she still finds time to help with her younger siblings and take on chores around the house, all while staying committed to her health. She's adamant about maintaining a healthy lifestyle, regularly hitting the gym and sticking to a nutritious diet, showing a maturity and dedication that fills me with joy.

Her ability to juggle so much at such a young age is nothing short of remarkable. She has big dreams of becoming a travel nurse, and I have no doubt that she will excel in whatever she sets her mind to. I will support her every step of the way, just as she has always supported me and our family. Her strength, resilience, and ambition make me incredibly proud, and I can't wait to see all the amazing things she will accomplish.

The younger three—Caiden, 11; Layla, 6; and Melody, 2—are still in the early stages of their journeys, with plenty of time before they're ready to face the world on their own. But even now, I'm committed to laying the foundation for their futures, planting the seeds of success that I hope will grow and flourish as they do.

For Caiden, who is just starting to navigate the transition from childhood to adolescence, I focus on teaching him the importance of hard work and perseverance. Whether it's through his schoolwork, his hobbies, or his responsibilities at home, I encourage him to give his best effort in everything he does. I want him to understand that success isn't handed to you; it's earned through dedication and determination.

Layla, with her bright curiosity and boundless energy, is at an age where her sense of responsibility is beginning to take shape. I try to nurture this by giving her small tasks that she can manage, reinforcing the idea that she has an important role in our family. Whether it's helping to set the table or taking care of her toys, I'm teaching her that being responsible is about taking care of the things and people you love.

And then there's Melody, the youngest, just 2 years old, with her whole life ahead of her. For her, it's about instilling kindness and empathy from the very beginning. I surround her with love, teaching her through example how to be gentle and caring, knowing that these early lessons will shape her character as she grows.

For all three of them, I try to introduce the concepts of hard work, responsibility, and kindness as early as possible. I know that these values will serve as their compass, guiding them through the challenges and opportunities life will bring. While they still have a while to go before they're ready to step out into the world, I'm confident that the seeds I'm planting now will help them grow into strong, capable, and compassionate individuals.

For a long time, I resisted the idea of being like my mom, determined to carve out my own path, separate from the struggles and challenges she faced. But as time passed, I've come to embrace the connection between us. My mother's resilience, her ability to survive and push forward despite overwhelming odds, has become my own strength.

She wasn't perfect, and her life was marked by mistakes that I vowed never to repeat. But even in her flaws, there were lessons—lessons in what not to do, yes, but also in the power of perseverance. Her determination to keep going, no matter how tough things got, is something I carry with me every day. It's a part of her that lives on through me and through the values I pass on to my children.

In these moments of reflection, I realize that the title of my journey—Fragments of Her, Pieces of Me—isn't just a phrase; it's the essence of who I am. My mother's life, her experiences, her strengths, and even her weaknesses have all shaped me into the person I am today. And as I continue to grow and learn, I see how those fragments of her life have become the pieces that make up mine, guiding me as I navigate my own path and pass on her legacy to the next generation.

In May of 2022, I welcomed my last child, Melody, into the world. Like her sibling Layla, she was born prematurely, arriving earlier than expected. However, what made Melody's birth even more poignant was the fact that she was the only one of my children who never had the chance to meet my mother before she passed away.

When I first went to visit Melody in the NICU, I was filled with a mix of emotions—relief that she was here, worry about her fragile state, and an overwhelming sadness that my mother wasn't there to share this moment with me. As I approached Melody's incubator, something immediately caught my eye—a large picture above her, showcasing a stunning blue butterfly. The vibrant image seemed to glow with a life of its own, its presence so unexpected and yet so deeply comforting.

In that instant, I felt a wave of peace wash over me. I realized that this butterfly was more than just a decoration in the NICU; it was a message from my mother. It was her way of telling me that although she was no longer here on earth, she would always be with me in spirit. The blue butterfly symbolized her enduring presence, a gentle reminder that her love and guidance would forever surround me and my children.

It was as if she was reassuring me from beyond, letting me know that while her earthly journey had ended, her connection to us would never fade. That butterfly became a symbol of the eternal bond between us—a bond that transcends life and death, one that will carry on in the hearts of my children and me for as long as we live.

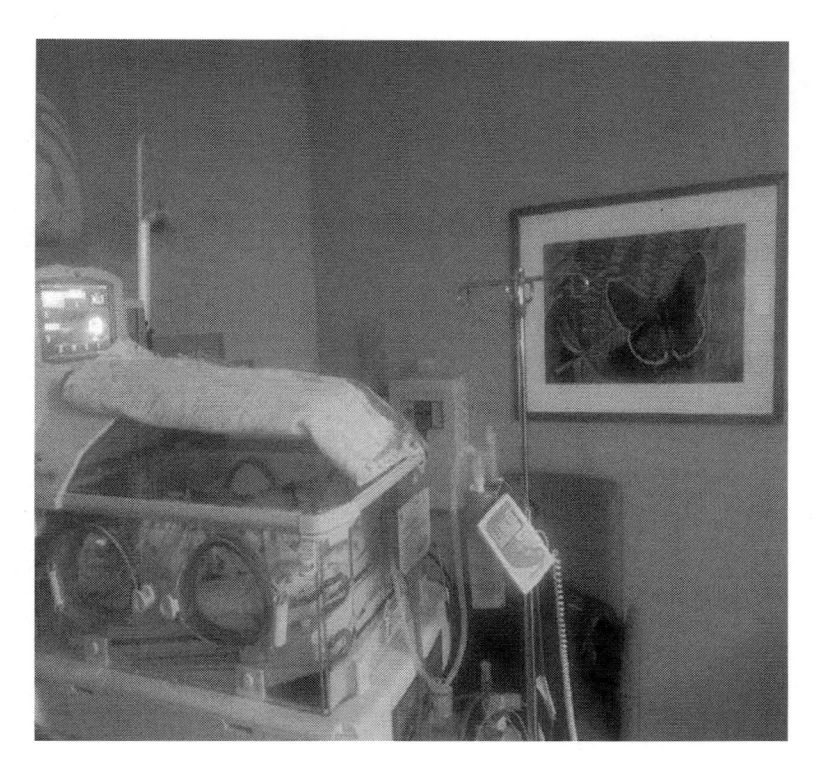

Figure 1 Melody's NICU room at Temple Baylor Scott and White Hospital, Temple TX

About the Author

Candice is a resilient mother of five and a passionate storyteller, whose life journey has been marked by challenges, growth, and an unwavering dedication to family. Born in Chicago, Il and raised in Minneapolis, MN, Candice navigated the complexities of early motherhood, balancing multiple jobs and schooling while striving to provide a better life for her children. Her experiences have shaped her into a person of deep empathy, strength, and insight.

In her memoir, Fragments of Her, Pieces of Me, Candice delves into the profound impact of her upbringing, exploring the ways in which her mother's life and choices influenced her own. With a candid voice, she reflects on the cycles of trauma, resilience, and transformation that have defined her path. Through her writing, Candice offers a heartfelt and raw account of what it means to break generational patterns, embrace vulnerability, and find strength in unexpected places.

Candice's memoir is not just a story of survival—it's a testament to the power of love, the importance of self-discovery, and the enduring bond between a mother and her children. With a keen eye for detail and an honest approach to life's complexities, she invites readers to join her on a journey of healing, forgiveness, and growth.

When she's not writing, Candice is deeply involved in her community, organizing book donations for local NICUs in honor of NICU Awareness Month. She is also a devoted advocate for Melody's Little Library, using her voice and experiences to uplift and inspire others.

Candice currently resides in Texas with her children, where she continues to write, nurture her family, and cherish the fragments of her past that have shaped her into the person she is today.